EAT WELL FOR A POUND

BY
JUDY WILLIAMS

Harlequin Books Limited.
First published in Great Britain in 1993 by Harlequin Books Ltd.

Copyright © 1993 Harlequin Books Limited.

ISBN 1 897757 01 8

Printed and bound in Great Britain

Barn Oast, Woodfalls Industrial Estate, Gravelly Way,
Laddingford, Kent ME18 6DA

HARLEQUIN
BOOKS LIMITED

CONTENTS

ACKNOWLEDGEMENTS

Photography by David Jordan
Food and props styling by Judy Williams
Thanks to The Pier Trading Company, Tottenham Court
Road, London W1, for loaning photographic props.

All recipes featured
in this book are designed
to serve four people.

Eat Well!

INTRODUCTION

Food, glorious food, you just can't beat it, and neither should the recent recession! Some folks spend more on a mediocre meal in a restaurant than you need to spend in a week to feed the family like royalty.

Having to watch every penny could make meals boring but this book won't allow you to slip into bad habits. Cooking and eating should be fun, fun, fun no matter how much money you spend. So don't go for broke go for bargains.

All supermarkets and shops have special offers and making the most of them is essential for the penny-wise cook! It's easy to get stuck in a rut, buying the same things every week, but as a serious shopper, you can adjust the week's menus to suit the super savers you find.

Plan ahead. Work out a weekly menu, write a shopping list and stick to it. But think creatively, think cheap - swap vegetables if sprouts are on special offer, use a can of pears instead of peaches and Edam instead of Cheddar if it's reduced.

This is just one of the shopping skills we need to stretch the pounds and make the cash go further.

But there are plenty of other ways to save money too.

★ Save all the money off tokens printed in papers and on packets.

★ Eat before you shop. A rumbling tum will succumb to the tempting smells from the bakeries and make you buy more than you need.

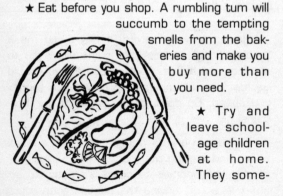

★ Try and leave school-age children at home. They somehow manage to add pounds to the shopping bill by slipping things to try into the trolley.

★ Fruit and veg may be cheaper bought from market stalls but if you can't choose it yourself, you have to take a chance with the quality. Seasonal stuff in plentiful supply is always better value.

A GOOD DEAL BETTER

We all love a bargain, and making the most of your money is the key to stress-free shopping and housekeeping success. Spending wisely but well is only the beginning, learning how to transform your shopping into fabulous feasts for the family is the next step.

TEN POINT PLAN

1 Make meals last two days. A hot roast chicken one day becomes cold chicken, jacket potatoes and salad the next. And to make you feel really thrifty boil up the bones to make stock for soup.

2 Cut cake style desserts into eight and serve two days running, or as a lunchbox treat.

3 Cheap meals don't have to be boring. Adding curry powder to mince, soy sauce to chicken dishes and chopped fresh herbs to pasta will transform an ordinary dish into an exotic repast. Okay, so the kids hate spicy food! Split the mixture and spice up the adults' half.

4 Involve the whole family in your cooking. The family that cooks together has fun together! Always remembering the kitchen can be a dangerous place, get the kids to chop the softer vegetables, grate cheese or make a salad dressing (depending on their age, of course, although even toddlers like to stir batter or play with pastry.) How else are they going to learn to cook?

5 Cooking and eating should be pleasurable, not a chore to 'get over and done with' before getting the kids off to bed. Try to fit TV programmes around meal times so the family eat together.

6 When two incomes drop to one through redundancy or pregnancy it's time to change those extravagant shopping habits. Cut down on ready-cooked meals, finely chopped onions and exotic vegetables. It's back to honest-to-goodness grub, just as scrummy but kinder to your purse.

7 Shop weekly to snap up the best money-off bargains, and to vary the menu as much as possible.

8 Think of the dreaded fuel bills!

★ Plan meals that don't need oven, grill and hob on at the same time.

★ Put the casserole with the jacket spuds in the oven together.

★ It is possible to put vegetables in a roasting tin with a little water, cover with foil and cook them in the oven too.

★ Put the spuds in a saucepan and steam the veggies in a colander over the top to save fuel.

9 Shopping later in the day can lead to a treasure trove. Dairy produce, meat and bread are often reduced for a quick sale. Watch out for stuff that has reached it's sell-by date and is going for knock-down prices.

10 Some experts think that supermarket shoppers who start at the far end of the shop and work backwards spend less. Give it a try, the experts may be right this time!

COOK'S POINTERS

★ The flavourings and seasonings used in recipes are approximate and can be adjusted to suit individual taste.

★ Onions and garlic cloves are assumed to be medium-sized.

★ All ovens cook at slightly different rates and cooking times may vary, especially if there is more than one dish in the oven at a time.

★ All food should go into a hot oven, so make sure you allow 15-20 mins for it to reach temperature.

★ The weights are stated in imperial and the approximate equivalent is in metric.

★ There's an approximate cost at the end of each recipe but prices will vary according to seasons and normal fluctuations in food prices.

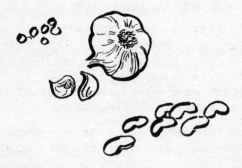

STOCKING THE STORECUPBOARD

It's pointless paying out pounds on a store cupboard mountain. Just stick to the essentials and a few extras in case a school pal stays or an unexpected auntie turns up. All food, even cans, should come date-stamped and used in strict rotation. Keep dry goods and cans a cool dark place, not next to the central heating boiler!.

Put this lot in your store cupboard and you'll never be at a loss.

Canned tomatoes; look out for the ones with onions and peppers, or herbs. They are a couple of pence more to buy but mean not having to add the extras.

Tomato puree; bought by the tube and really adds flavour. Store in the fridge after opening.

Canned sweetcorn; plenty of fibre and bulk to add to mince, salads and pizzas.

Baked beans; a meal in themselves, but add bulk to mince and casseroles.

Chick peas; handy for salads, casseroles and vegetable stews and lasagne.

Kidney beans; add 1 tsp chilli powder and beans to mince mixture to make a quick chilli con carne mixture to serve with rice or top jacket spuds.

Spaghetti in tomato sauce; quick snacks for kids and to mix into meat and vegetable dishes

Tuna in brine or oil; top pizzas, salads, jackets, sandwiches or stir into pasta.

Instant mash; saves time and fuel when making shepherd's or fish pie.

Rice; Basmati, if you can run to it, or easy cook, and pudding rice.

Red lentils; mix with mince for shepherd's pie or use on their own for lasagne. Need plenty of seasoning like mince.

Pasta; assorted dried pasta shapes to serve in sauce as a main meal or to bulk out meat or vegetable dishes.

Flour; plain for pastry and batter. Self-raising for cakes and desserts. Cornflour for thickening sauces .

Cereals and porridge oats; for toppings and cakes. Cereals also make a good late night snack!

Sugar; granulated, caster and soft brown or demerara.

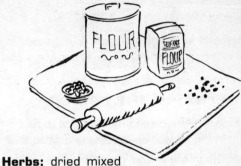

Herbs; dried mixed herbs or Italian mixed herbs.

Spices; Ground coriander, cumin, ginger, chilli, cinnamon and nutmeg, as well as a couple of different curry powders or pastes.

Oil, vinegar and coarse grain mustard; for frying, flavouring and dressings.

Soy sauce; for stir fries, salads and to add extra flavour to gravies.

Assorted stock cubes; available in all sorts of meaty flavours as well as vegetable.

Salt and black pepper; use coarsely ground black peppercorns if possible.

Other useful things to stock are Ready to Serve custard or sachets of custard powder, a couple of chutneys or pickles, coffee and cocoa powder, trifle sponges, jellies and instant whip desserts to keep the kids happy.

FILLING THE FRIDGE

All dairy produce and meat needs to be stored in the fridge. Vegetables and salad stuff also keeps longer if they're chilled, as do fruit juices and salad dressings.

Long-life cream ; usually slightly cheaper than real cream and keeps longer. Handy for pasta sauces, desserts and pouring. Use double or whipping cream for best all round use.

Natural yogurt; fabulous poured over fresh fruit or cereal, makes super salad dressings, lighter cakes and splendid sauces for pasta when mixed with a little cream. Stir into soups and curries just before serving.

Cheese; keep your favourite type in stock for grating into soup or sauces, and over pasta and crumbles. Slice thinly for sandwiches and toast. Take advantage of the cheesey specials on offer at the deli counter at your local supermarket.

Grated Parmesan cheese; slightly more expensive but you don't need much. Adds extra tang to sauces and toppings.

Cold meats; useful for sarnies, but also on toast with poached eggs or snipped into omelettes, pasta sauces, or over pizzas.

Raw meat; Unwrap that Sunday joint as soon as possible, rinse off any blood and and cover loosely before chilling. Remove any giblets from a chicken as soon as it has defrosted.

FOR THE FREEZER

If you aren't too sure about what can be frozen or how long things keep, pop into the local library and check out one of the specialist books. The freezer comes into it's own as a place

to keep standby stuff, in case of emergencies and to freeze your own produce for use later in the year

Ready made puff pastry; for savoury and sweet dishes

Frozen peas or beans; tip them into stews or salads, or serve with the main meal. Often one of the few green vegetables kids will actually eat.

Minced beef; one of the most versatile meats to stock. Turn it into meatballs, burgers, rissoles, lasagnes, shepherd's pies etc etc. It is often on special offer too.

Chicken thighs or pieces; only cook when thoroughly defrosted. Cook on the bone for casseroles and barbecues, or cut the meat off for kebabs

Spinach; packed full of iron and delicious made into roulades or stuffing.

Bread; stock sliced loaves, crumpets, muffins, rolls and part-baked bread.

Pancakes; make a few extra and toss them onto a pile with a sheet of greaseproof between each one, wrap and freeze.

Ice cream; even the 1 litre vanilla blocks are handy for quick desserts for kids. Top with chocolate icing, honey or warmed jam.

Look out for offers on individual mini-pizzas, sausages that can be cooked from frozen and other quick-to-cook things for kids.

TIP: Whizz stale bread in a processor, or dice finely, and freeze. Add to mince when making meatballs or burgers Grate ends of cheese and freeze ready to scatter over lasagnes, savoury crumbles, quiches or pizza. Mix with breadcrumbs to go even further,

Freeze left over wine in ice cube trays and add to stocks and sauces when needed.

EQUIPMENT

Slow cooker

Can be left to casserole meat while you are out all day, but will need everything prepared in the morning. If you don't have one pop the meat, veg and stock into a dish with a tight fitting lid and cook at 110C/225F/Gas 1/4.

Microwave

Food never tastes quite the same when cooked in a microwave oven but it can cook or reheat things quickly, which is ideal for the family that eats at different times. There are several different types available now so check out which one suits you best.

Pressure cooker

Cooks vegetables and tougher meat much quicker than a conventional oven. Ideal for steamed savoury and sweet puds as well.

Wok

Chinese food is fast growing in popularity and more people own a wok now than ever before. But don't panic if you fancy having a go and haven't got one. A large frying pan will do almost as well.

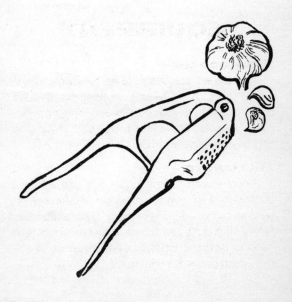

CHAPTER ONE
SOUPERBOWLS

There can't be a simpler meal to get together than home made soup. Stock can be made from boiling up bones left from a joint and odd fresh vegetables found in the fridge can be used as flavouring. Don't ignore canned and frozen veggies either, and those invaluable stock cubes, costing around 10p each, now available in so many flavours, including vegetable. Use one for each pint of stock required.

Canned soups, good as they are cannot compare to a good homemade one, but can be jazzed up with interesting spices, fried onions or garlic croutons. You could even try experimenting and mixing two different types together!

A bowl of hot, hearty soup, topped with grated cheese served with warm crusty bread always makes a welcome and filling meal.

Whether you prefer the thinner, smoother type or soup with chunks of vegetables, meat and pasta, you are sure to find a recipe here that will suit.

Croutons: Remove crusts from two slices of bread and cut into small squares. Heat oil and shallow-fry bread until crisp and brown.

Drain on kitchen paper.

SNACK SOUPS

Making thinner, lighter soups, suitable for snacks or starters is really easy, and can be very cheap. Follow the three simple steps to successful soup every time, none of which will cost you more than £2 for four people.

1. Sweat, or fry, the vegetables in a little oil or butter without browning. This will enhance the flavour of your soup.

2. Add liquid and simmer until vegetables are tender.

3. Smooth to a puree. Use a processor or liquidiser for a smoother soup, or a potato masher for a coarser texture.

CARROT AND CORIANDER SOUP

1 tbsp oil
1 onion, chopped
1lb/450g carrots, peeled and chopped
4oz/100g potatoes, peeled and chopped
1 1/2 pints/ 900ml chicken stock
salt and pepper
2 tsp ground coriander
2 tbsp orange juice
1/2 pint / 300ml milk

METHOD

1. Heat the oil in a pan and fry the onions until softened. Add chopped carrots and potatoes and fry for 4-5 mins. stirring occasionally.

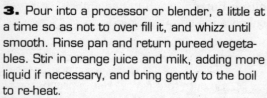

2. Add stock, seasonings and coriander. Bring to the boil and simmer for 20-30 mins, until the vegetables are really tender.

3. Pour into a processor or blender, a little at a time so as not to over fill it, and whizz until smooth. Rinse pan and return pureed vegetables. Stir in orange juice and milk, adding more liquid if necessary, and bring gently to the boil to re-heat.

Approx. cost £1.10

CURRIED PARSNIP SOUP

1 tbsp oil
1 onion, chopped
1lb/450g parsnips, peeled and chopped
8oz/225g carrots, peeled and chopped
2 tsp medium curry powder (according to taste)
1 tsp ground cumin
2 pints/1 litre chicken stock
salt and pepper
4 tbsp single cream

METHOD

1. Heat oil and fry onions until softened. Add chopped parsnips and carrots and fry for 5 mins, stirring occasionally.

2. Stir in curry powder and cumin and mix well. Add stock and seasonings and bring to the boil. Simmer gently for 30-40 mins until tender.

3. Pour into liquidiser or processor and whizz until smooth. Return to rinsed pan and reheat. Transfer to soup bowls, add a spoonful of cream to each and stir through the soup before serving.

Approx cost £1.20

LEEK AND POTATO SOUP

1 tbsp oil
4 large leeks, washed and sliced
4 large potatoes, peeled and chopped
2 pints/1 litre chicken or vegetable stock
1 tsp grated nutmeg
salt and pepper
3 rashers streaky bacon

METHOD

1. Heat oil and fry leeks until softened. Add potatoes and cook for further 5 mins.
2. Add stock, nutmeg and seasonings and bring to the boil. Simmer for 20 mins, until vegetables are tender.
3. Pour soup into a liquidiser or processor and whizz until smooth. Return to rinsed-out pan and re-heat gently adding a little more water if necessary. Meanwhile grill bacon until crispy and snip into small pieces. Transfer soup to bowls and scatter bacon over the top before serving.
Approx cost £1.40

WATERCRESS AND CUCUMBER SOUP

1 tbsp oil
1 onion, chopped
1 cucumber, finely chopped
1 bunch watercress, rinsed - roughly chopped

1 pint/600ml chicken or vegetable stock
1 tbsp lemon juice
1 tsp nutmeg
salt and pepper
1/2 pint milk/300ml milk
2 tsp cornflour

METHOD
1. Heat oil and fry onion until softened. Add cucumber and watercress (reserve a few sprigs for decoration) and cook for further 5 mins.
2. Add stock, lemon juice, nutmeg and sea-sonings, bring to the boil and simmer for 15 mins.
3. Pour soup into a liquidiser or processor and whizz until smooth. Return to rinsed pan and re-heat gently. Add milk and bring back to the boil. Mix the cornflour with a little water and add to the soup, stirring all the time until thickened. Serve hot or chilled.
Approx cost £ 1.45

PEA SOUP

1 tbsp oil
1 onion, chopped
1 large potato, peeled and chopped
2lb/1kg bag frozen minty peas
2 pints/1 litre chicken or vegetable stock
salt and pepper
4 tbsp single or sour cream

METHOD

1. Heat oil and fry onion until softened. Add potato and fry for further 5 mins.

2. Add peas, stock and seasonings, bring to the boil and simmer for 20 mins, until potatoes are tender.

3. Pour into a liquidiser or processor and whizz until smooth. Return to rinsed pan and re-heat. Stir in a spoonful of cream before serving.

Approx cost £1.45

CELERY AND STILTON SOUP

2oz/50g butter or margarine
1 onion, chopped
4 sticks celery, chopped
2oz/50g plain flour
2 pints/1 litre chicken or vegetable stock
salt and pepper
4oz/100g Stilton cheese

METHOD

1. Melt butter in a pan and fry onion and celery for 5 mins, until softened.

2. Lower the heat and stir in flour. Gradually add the stock, a little at a time, beating well after each addition. Bring to the boil and simmer for 20-25 mins.

3. Pour the soup into a liquidiser or processor, a little at a time, and whizz until smooth. Return to rinsed pan and bring back gently to the boil. Crumble the Stilton into the soup, allow to melt slightly and serve topped with croutons.

Approx cost £1.40

BEETROOT AND APPLE SOUP

1 tbsp oil
2 onions, chopped
1 1/2lb/675g raw beetroot, peeled and diced
2 cooking apples, quartered, peeled and chopped
2 pints/1 litre beef stock
2 tbsp lemon juice
5 tbsp sherry (optional)
4 tbsp sour cream

METHOD

1. Heat oil and fry onions until softened. Add beetroot and apple and fry for further 2 mins.

2. Add stock and bring to the boil. Simmer for 45 mins, until vegetables are tender.

3. Pour soup into a liquidiser or processor and whizz until smooth. Return to rinsed pan and add lemon juice and sherry. Serve warm or chilled with a swirl of soured cream stirred through.

Approx cost £1.35

TIP: Finely dice the beetroot so it cooks more quickly.

TOMATO AND VEGETABLE SOUP

1 tbsp oil
2 onions, chopped
3 carrots, peeled and chopped
1 small turnip, peeled and diced
3 sticks celery, chopped
1 pint/600ml chicken stock
1 14oz/397g can chopped tomatoes
1 tsp dried mixed herbs
salt and pepper

METHOD

1. Heat oil and fry onions until softened. Add carrots, turnip and celery and fry for further 5 mins, stirring occasionally.

2. Add stock, tomatoes, herbs and seasonings and bring to the boil. Reduce heat and simmer for 20-30 mins, until veggies are tender.

3. Pour soup into a liquidiser or processor, in small quantities, and whizz until smooth. Serve hot

Approx cost £1.20

BACON AND LENTIL SOUP

4oz/100g red lentils
1 tbsp oil
2 leeks, sliced
1 clove garlic, crushed
1 carrot, peeled and chopped
1 small turnip, peeled and diced
8 rashers rindless streaky bacon, chopped
2 pints/1 litre ham or chicken stock
1 tsp dried mixed herbs
salt and pepper

METHOD

1. Put lentils in a bowl, cover with cold water and leave to soak overnight.

Heat oil and fry leeks and garlic until softened. Add chopped carrot and turnip

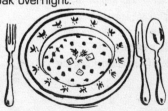

11

and fry for 3 mins before adding chopped
bacon and frying for further 4-5 mins.
2. Rinse and drain lentils and add to pan with
the stock, herbs and seasonings, Bring to the
boil and simmer for an hour.
3. Pour soup into a liquidiser or processor, a
little at a time, and whizz until smooth. Return
to rinsed pan and re-heat gently. before serving.
Approx cost £1.70

TIP: Use canned lentils for extra speed.

MULLIGATAWNY SOUP
1oz/25g butter
1 onion, chopped
2 carrots, peeled and chopped
1 small swede, peeled and diced
1 small dessert apple, peeled and chopped
4 rashers rindless streaky bacon, chopped
1oz/25g plain flour
1 tbsp medium curry paste
2 tbsp tomato puree
1 tbsp mango chutney (optional)
2 pints/1 litre beef stock
1 tsp dried mixed herbs
salt and pepper
2oz/50g basmati rice

METHOD

1. Melt butter in a pan and fry onions, carrots, swede, apple and bacon until lightly
browned.

2. Add flour, curry paste, tomato puree and
chutney and fry for 2 mins. Add stock, herbs,
and seasonings and bring to the boil. Simmer
for 35 mins.

3. Pour the soup, a little at a time, into a liquidiser or processor and whizz until smooth.
Return to rinsed pan and bring back to the
boil. Add rice and simmer for 12 mins, until
cooked. Serve hot

Approx cost £1.70

CREAMY MUSHROOM SOUP

1 tbsp oil
1 onion, chopped
1 clove garlic, crushed
1lb/450g mushrooms, wiped and chopped
2 pints/1 litre chicken or vegetable stock
1 large potato, peeled and grated
salt and pepper
¼ pint/125ml double cream

METHOD

1. Heat oil and fry onion and garlic until softened. Add mushrooms and fry for 5 mins, until
starting to brown.

2. Add stock, grated potato and seasonings

and bring to the boil. Simmer for 10-15 mins, until potatoes are tender.

3. Pour soup into a liquidiser or processor, a little at a time, and whizz until smooth. Return to rinsed pan and re-heat gently. Stir in cream just before serving.

Approx cost £2.00

FENNEL SOUP

1oz/25g butter
1 onion, chopped
1 large fennel bulb, washed and chopped
1 1/2 pints/ 900ml chicken stock
1 tsp dried mixed herbs
2 egg yolks
1/4 pint/125ml double cream
salt and pepper

METHOD

1. Melt butter in a pan and fry onion until softened. Add fennel and fry until starting to brown.

2. Add stock and herbs and bring to the boil. Simmer for 30-40 mins, until fennel is very tender.

3. Pour stock into a liquidiser or processor, a little at a a time, and whizz until smooth. Return to rinsed pan and re-heat gently. Mix eggs and cream together in a small bowl. Add a spoonful of soup to this mixture and stir.

Pour this mixture back into the pan very slowly, stirring all the time. Do not allow the soup to boil or it will curdle. Season to taste and serve immediately.

Approx cost £1.80

CREAM OF CELERY SOUP

1oz/25g butter
6 stalks celery, chopped
1 large potato, peeled and diced
2 leeks, chopped
1 1/2 pints/900ml chicken stock
1/4 pint/125ml single cream
1/4 pint/125ml milk
salt and pepper

METHOD

1. Melt butter in a pan and fry celery, potato and leeks for 5 mins until starting to soften.

2. Add stock and bring to the boil. Simmer for 25-30 mins until vegetables are really tender.

3. Pour soup, a little at a time, into a liquidiser or processor and whizz until smooth. Return to rinsed pan and re-heat gently, after stirring in the cream and milk. Season well and serve piping hot.

Approx cost £ 1.75

TOMATO AND BASIL SOUP

1 tbsp olive oil
1 onion, chopped
1 clove garlic, crushed
1 medium potato, peeled and diced
1 1/2lb/ 675g ripe tomatoes, quartered
1 pint/600ml chicken or vegetable stock
2 tbsp chopped fresh basil
salt and pepper

METHOD

1. Heat oil and fry
onion and garlic
until softened. Add
potatoes and fry for further 15
mins, until spuds are cooked but
not browned.

2. Add tomatoes and cook for 2 mins before adding stock. Bring to the boil and simmer for 20 mins. Pour soup through a large sieve to remove all pips and skin and return to rinsed pan.

3. Add chopped basil and seasonings and re-heat gently before serving. It is also delicious served cold.

Approx cost £1.80

TIP: When fresh tomatoes are expensive use a 397g can chopped ones instead. A good way to use up that glut of homegrown ones too!

CHEESE AND ONION SOUP

1 oz/25g butter
2 onions, chopped
1 clove garlic, crushed
2 sticks celery, chopped
1oz/25g plain flour
1 pint/600ml milk
1/2 pint/300ml chicken stock
1/2 tsp ground nutmeg
salt and pepper
2 thick slices bread
4oz/100g grated cheese

METHOD

1. Melt butter and fry onions, garlic and celery until softened, but not browned.

2. Add flour and stir well. Gradually add the milk, a little at a time, beating well after each addition. Add stock, spices and seasonings and bring to the boil, stirring all the time. Simmer for 5 mins.

3. Pour soup into a liquidiser or blender, a little at a time, and whizz until smooth. Return to rinsed pan and reheat gently, stirring occasionally. Meanwhile toast the bread on both sides. Scatter half the cheese over, brown under the grill and cut into small squares. Remove soup from the heat, stir in remaining cheese and sprinkle the cheesey croutons over the top.

Approx cost £1.60

MAIN MEAL SOUPS

CHICKEN AND SWEETCORN SOUP

1 tbsp oil
3 spring onions, finely chopped
2 large potatoes, peeled and diced
2 tbsp medium curry paste
1 11oz/326g can sweetcorn niblets
1 pint/600ml chicken stock
1 pint/600ml milk
2 tbsp cornflour
1 chicken breast, cooked and diced
salt and pepper

METHOD

Heat oil and fry onion and potato for 10-12
mins, until starting to soften, but not brown.
Add curry paste and mix well.
Add sweetcorn and stock and bring to the boil.
Simmer for 10-15 mins. Add milk. Mix corn-
flour with a little cold water and add to the
soup, stirring all the time.
Add chicken and simmer for further 3 mins.
Season well and serve piping hot with prawn
crackers.
Approx cost £ 2.00

FRENCH ONION SOUP

2 tbsp oil
2oz/50g butter
1 1/2lbs/675g onions, thinly sliced
2 cloves garlic, crushed
2 pints/1 litre beef stock
1/4 pint/125ml white wine
salt and pepper
1 small French stick
4oz/100g grated cheese

METHOD

Heat oil and butter together in a pan and fry
onion and garlic together until very browned ,
but not burnt. Add stock and wine and bring
soup to the boil.
Season well and simmer for 20-25 mins.

Cut the French stick into $1/2$ inch/1 cm slices
and toast on both sides. Sprinkle cheese over
each one and brown under the grill. Serve
soup with toasted slices on top.
Approx cost £2.00

CHILLI BEAN SOUP

1 tbsp oil
1 onion, chopped
1 clove garlic, crushed
4oz/100g minced beef
1 397g can chopped tomatoes with onions
and peppers
1 pint/600ml beef stock
2 tbsp tomato puree
1 tsp dried mixed Italian herbs
salt and pepper
1 220g can kidney beans

METHOD

Heat oil and fry onion and garlic until softened.
Add mince and fry until browned all over. Add
chopped tomatoes, stock, puree, herbs and
seasonings and simmer for 25-30 mins, until
cooked and reduced slightly. Add kidney beans
and cook for further 5 mins to heat through.
Serve with crusty bread.
Approx cost £ 1.50

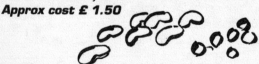

COCK-A LEEKIE SOUP

1 oz/25g butter
2 leeks, washed and sliced
2 chicken joints, defrosted
2 pints chicken stock or water
2 tsp dried mixed herbs
1 bay leaf
salt and pepper
3oz/75g prunes (optional)

METHOD

Melt butter and fry leeks for 5 mins. Put into a
saucepan with the chicken joints, stock, herbs,
bay leaf and seasoning.
Bring to the boil, reduce heat and simmer for
1-1 ¼ hours. Add prunes and cook for further
20 mins. Lift the chicken out of soup, remove
and shred the meat. Return chicken meat to
the pan, check seasonings and serve with granary baps.
Approx cost £1.50

CHICKEN NOODLE SOUP

2 pints chicken stock, preferably from boiling
bones and vegetables
3oz/75g fine egg noodles
1 tbsp lemon juice
salt and pepper
2 tbsp chopped fresh parsley

METHOD

Heat the stock in a large pan and add the noodles when boiling.

Simmer for 3-5 mins, until tender before adding lemon juice, seasonings and parsley.

Serve hot with warm bread.

Approx cost 90p

MINESTRONE SOUP

1 tbsp oil
1 onion, sliced
1 clove garlic, crushed
2 carrots, peeled and sliced
2 sticks celery, sliced
1 397g can chopped tomatoes with herbs
1 1/2 pints/900ml vegetable stock
1 397g can cooked haricot beans
4oz/100g cabbage, shredded
4oz/100g short cut macaroni
salt and pepper

METHOD

Heat oil and fry onion and garlic until softened. Add sliced carrots and celery and fry for further 5 mins. Add chopped tomatoes and stock and simmer for 15 mins. Add beans, cabbage, macaroni and seasonings and cook for further 15 mins, until pasta is tender, adding more liquid if necessary.

Serve piping hot with bread.

Approx cost £1.75

VEGETABLE AND BREAD SOUP

6oz/175g green lentils
8 rashers rindless streaky bacon, chopped
8oz/225g frozen broad beans
8oz/225g frozen peas
4oz/100g green cabbage,
shredded
salt and pepper
8 thin slices bread

METHOD

Wash lentils, put in a pan, cover with water
and simmer for 45 mins. Reserve liquor and
put lentils into a liquidiser or processor and
whizz until smooth. Return to rinsed pan with
cooking liquor. Add bacon and vegetables and
bring to the boil. Add seasonings and simmer
for 20-35 mins, until vegetables are tender.
Line the soup bowls with the slices of bread
and pour soup over to serve.
Approx cost £2.00

TIP: Look out for bacon off-cuts at the deli
counter.

PASTA AND VEGETABLE SOUP

1 tbsp oil
6 rashers streaky bacon, chopped
1 onion, sliced
2 cloves garlic, crushed

6oz/175g courgettes, sliced
1 397g can chopped tomatoes with herbs
1 pint beef or vegetable stock
6oz/175g dried pasta shapes
salt and pepper
2 tbsp grated Parmesan cheese

METHOD

Heat oil and fry bacon, onion and garlic until
just starting to brown. Add courgettes and fry
for further 2 mins. Add chopped tomatoes and
stock and simmer for 10mins. Add pasta
shapes and seasonings and cook for further
10-15 mins, until pasta is tender. Serve hot
with a sprinkling of Parmesan cheese and
crispy rolls or breadsticks.

Approx cost £1.90

RATATOUILLE SOUP

1 tbsp oil
1 onion, thinly sliced
2 cloves garlic, crushed
2 courgettes, sliced
1 red or green pepper, de-seeded and sliced
1 small aubergine, sliced
1 397g can chopped tomatoes with herbs
1 pint chicken or vegetable stock
2 tbsp tomato puree
salt and pepper

METHOD

Heat oil and fry onion and garlic until starting to brown. Add courgettes, pepper and aubergine and stir-fry for 4-5 mins. Add chopped tomatoes, stock puree and seasonings, bring to the boil and simmer for 20-30 mins. Serve hot with garlic bread.

Approx cost £2.00

THICK COUNTRY VEGETABLE

2oz/50g butter
1 onion, chopped
4 carrots, peeled and chopped
2 leeks, thickly sliced
4 sticks celery, sliced
8oz/225g cauliflower, broken into small florets
4 large potatoes, peeled and diced
2pints/1litre vegetable stock
salt and pepper
1/2 bunch watercress, chopped

METHOD

Melt butter in a pan and fry onions, carrots, leeks and celery for 5 mins. Lower heat and add cauliflower and potatoes. Stir fry for 3 mins. before pouring stock over. Season well, bring to the boil and

simmer for 20-30 mins, until vegetables are tender, adding more liquid if necessary. Add chopped watercress and serve hot with warm bread.

Approx cost £ 2.00

CREAMY CAULIFLOWER SOUP

1 large cauliflower, cut into small florets
1 onion, chopped
2oz/50g butter
2oz/50g plain flour
3/4 pint/450ml milk
2 tbsp tomato puree
2 tsp dried mixed herbs
salt and pepper
1 tsp ground nutmeg
1 egg yolk
4tbsp single or sour cream

METHOD

Put cauliflower florets and chopped onion in a pan of boiling water and simmer until tender. Drain, but reserve 3/4pint/450ml of water. Put half the cauliflower into a liquidiser or processor and whizz until smooth. Reserve the other half.

Melt butter in a large pan and stir in flour. Add the milk and reserved cooking liquid a little at a time, beating well after each addition and bring to the boil, stirring all the time until mixture thickens. Add whole cauliflower pieces, puree, herbs and seasonings. Bring to the boil gently. Mix egg yolk with cream in a small bowl. Add a spoonful of the soup and stir well. Slowly add egg mixture to soup, stirring all the time. Do not allow to boil or the soup will curdle. Serve hot.

Approx cost £1.90

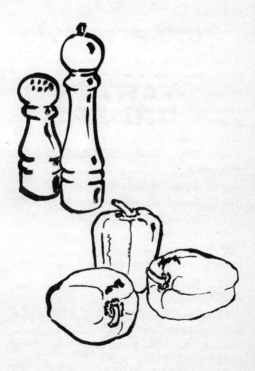

27

CHAPTER TWO
UNDER STARTER'S ORDERS

TOMATO AND MOZZARELLA SALAD

2 beef tomatoes, sliced
4oz/100g Mozzarella cheese, thinly sliced
2 spring onions, finely chopped
2 tbsp olive oil
1oz/25g black olives
freshly ground black pepper

METHOD

Arrange sliced tomatoes and cheese in alternate layers on four individual plates. Scatter the chopped onions and olives over. Trickle the

oil over each salad and grind black pepper on top. Serve at room temperature, garnished with fresh basil if desired.
Approx cost £1.95

CHICKEN LIVER PATE

8oz/225g frozen chicken livers, defrosted
1 small onion, chopped
¼ pint/150ml double cream
2 tbsp tomato puree
salt and pepper
4 slices thin cut bread

METHOD

Gently fry chicken livers and chopped onion until cooked. Remove from heat and allow to cool before pouring into a liquidiser or processor and whizzing until smooth. Add cream, tomato puree and seasonings and whizz again. Transfer to four ramekin dishes or one large dish and chill.
Toast the bread on both sides and cut each slice into eight fingers.Serve warm with the paté.
Approx cost 90p

STUFFED MUSHROOMS

4 large mushrooms
2oz/50g butter
1 small onion, finely sliced

1 carrot, cut into fine matchsticks
2 sticks celery, cut into fine matchsticks
2 tbsp soy sauce
1 tsp ground ginger
salt and pepper
1 170g can crabmeat in
brine

METHOD

Cut off mushroom stalks
and chop them finely. Melt the butter in a frying pan and gently fry the whole mushroom
caps until softened and lightly brown. Lift out
and keep warm. Add onions and carrots to the
pan and fry for 2-3 mins, until softened. Add
celery , chopped mushroom stalks and seasonings and cook until tender. Add crab and stir
gently together until heated through.
Arrange the mushroom caps on plates and
share crab mixture between them. Serve
immediately.
Approx cost £2.20

CRISPY POTATO SKINS AND DIP

8 large potatoes
oil for brushing
salt and pepper
6 tbsp mayonnaise
2 tbsp tartare sauce

METHOD

Scrub the spuds, prick with a fork and bake in the oven at 190C/375F/Gas 5 for 45 mins. Remove from oven and cut each spud into quarters. Use a sharp knife to scoop out some of the centre and return the skins to the roasting tin. Brush with oil and return to the oven. Cook for further 30-45 mins, until brown and crispy, brushing with oil once or twice during cooking time.

To make the dip, mix the mayonnaise and tartare sauce together and turn into a small bowl.

Arrange the skins around the dip and serve.

Approx cost £ 1.25

TIP: Save the scooped out spud to mix with tuna for fritters, or stir into a hash for tomorrow's tuck.

FRIED CHEESE

4 individual triangles of Camembert cheese
1 egg, beaten
2oz/50g fresh breadcrumbs
1/2 small onion, finely chopped
oil for shallow frying

METHOD

Cut each cheese triangle into three equal pieces.

Put beaten egg into one shallow bowl and breadcrumbs and chopped onions into another. Dip each cheese slice into egg and breadcrumbs twice.

Heat oil in a frying pan and shallow fry the cheese slices until crisp and browned. Serve immediately with a salad garnish.

Approx cost £ 1.75

TIP: Also works well with slices of Brie. Cook in hot oil so the outside crisps quickly.

PEPPERED EGGS

4 eggs
2 tbsp mayonnaise
1/2 tsp paprika
salt and pepper
1 tomato
8 small lettuce leaves

METHOD

Hard boil the eggs, rinse in cold water and shell. Scoop out yolks and put in a small bowl. Add the mayonnaise, paprika and seasonings. Beat until smooth and creamy before putting into a piping bag fitted with a large star nozzle.

Pipe a large rosette into the

centre of each egg. Sprinkle with a little paprika. Cut the tomato into thin wedges and
arrange on four small plates with the lettuce.
Stand eggs among salad and serve.
Approx cost 95p

INDIVIDUAL LEEK FLANS
8oz/225g plain flour
4oz/100g butter or margarine, cut into small
pieces
4oz/100g cheese, grated
1tbsp oil
2 leeks, thinly sliced
3 eggs, beaten
salt and pepper

METHOD
Put flour into a mixing bowl, add fat and rub in
with fingertips until mixture resembles fine
breadcrumbs. Add 2oz/50g of the cheese and
enough water to mix to a firm dough. Turn
onto a floured surface and knead lightly. Roll
out and use to line four 4inch/10cm individual
fluted flan rings. Prick bases with a fork, chill
for 20-30 mins before cooking at
190c/375F/Gas 5 for 15-20 mins, until lightly browned.
Meanwhile heat oil and fry sliced leeks until
softened and cooked. Share mixture between
the four flan cases.

Add a little water to beaten eggs and seasonings and pour over leeks. Top with remaining grated cheese and return to the oven for a further 15-20 mins, until set and browned. Serve warm with a salad garnish.

Approx cost £1.90

CHEESEY NACHOS

1 100g bag californian corn chips or Nachips
1/2 red pepper, de-seeded and finely diced
1/2 green pepper, de-seeded and finely diced
3oz/75g grated cheese
1 tsp chilli powder

METHOD

Arrange the Nachips on a heatproof plate. Scatter the chopped red and green peppers over. Top with grated cheese and sprinkle over the chilli powder. Put under a hot grill until cheese is melted and bubbling. Serve immediately.

Approx cost £1.90

FELAFELS WITH CUCUMBER RAITA

1 439g can cooked chick peas
1 egg, beaten
1 onion, finely chopped
2 cloves garlic, crushed
1 tsp ground cumin

1 tsp ground coriander
1/2 tsp chilli powder
salt and pepper
oil for shallow frying
1/4 pint/150ml natural yogurt
1/4 cucumber, finely chopped
2 sprigs chopped fresh mint

METHOD

Drain chick peas and tip into a bowl. Use a
potato masher to coarsely mash them before
adding egg, chopped onion, garlic and seasonings. Mix well and use hands to mould mixture
into walnut-sized balls and flatten slightly.
Heat oil and shallow fry felafels a few at a time
until browned all over. Drain on kitchen paper.
Put yogurt into a small bowl and stir in cucumber and mint. Mix well.
Share warm felafels between four plates with a
helping of raita and a salad garnish.
(Felafels can be made ahead and re-heated in
the oven before serving)
Approx cost £1.30

TIP: Add fresh
breadcrumbs if
the mixture is too
wet.

GUACAMOLE

2 ripe avocados
1 tbsp oil
1 tbsp lemon juice
1 clove garlic, crushed
2 large ripe tomatoes, finely chopped
1/2 small onion, thinly sliced
salt and pepper
tortilla chips

METHOD

Peel and roughly chop avocados. Put into a
bowl immediately with oil, lemon juice and garlic. Use a fork or potato masher to coarsely
mash them before adding the chopped tomatoes and sliced onion. Add seasonings and mix
well together. Keep tightly covered with cling
film until required. Serve with tortilla chips for
dipping.
Approx cost £2.00

RATATOUILLE ROLLS

1 small aubergine, cut into cubes
2 tbsp oil
1 onion, sliced
4 cloves garlic, crushed
2 courgettes, sliced
1 green pepper, de-
seeded and sliced
1 397g can chopped

tomatoes with herbs
salt and pepper
4 crusty rolls
2oz/50g butter

METHOD

Put chopped aubergine into a colander, sprinkle with salt and leave for 30 mins.

Heat oil and fry onion until softened. Add 2
crushed cloves of garlic and aubergines and fry
for 10 mins. Add courgettes, pepper, tomatoes and seasonings, cover and simmer for
20-30 mins, stirring occasionally.

Cut a slice off the top of the rolls to make a lid.
Hollow out the roll and reserve, or freeze,
breadcrumbs for another day. Beat butter until
soft, add remaining garlic and mix well. Spread
round the inside of the hollowed-out rolls and
on the inside of the 'lid'. Heat oven to
190c/375F/Gas 5 and cook rolls for 10-15
mins, until the butter has melted and the rolls
are hot. Put one on each plate and fill with hot
ratatouille mixture before serving.

Approx cost £2.00

LETTUCE WRAP

1 Iceberg lettuce
1 tbsp oil
1 onion, chopped
2 cloves garlic, crushed
8oz/225g minced beef
2oz/50g mushrooms, chopped
2 tbsp tomato puree
1 tbsp soy sauce
2 tsp chilli powder, adjust according to taste.
1 tsp dried mixed herbs
salt and pepper

METHOD

Run the lettuce under a cold tap to help separate leaves. Shake off excess water, pile leaves on a plate and chill.

Heat oil and fry onion and garlic until softened. Add mince and fry until browned all over. Add mushrooms and fry for further 3 mins. Drain off excess fat before adding puree, soy sauce, chilli powder, herbs and seasonings. Cook for 30-45 mins, until reduced and thickened.

Serve lettuce leaves and spicy mince mixture on separate plates. Put a spoonful of the meat mixture in the centre of a lettuce leaf and roll up like a parcel before eating with fingers.

***Approx cost
£2.00***

CHEESE AND MUSHROOM RAMEKINS

1 onion, finely chopped
8oz/225g streaky bacon, chopped
12oz/350g mushrooms, chopped
4oz/100g cream cheese
3 tbsp milk
salt and pepper
2oz/50g grated cheese
4 tbsp fresh breadcrumbs

METHOD

Fry chopped onion and bacon together until lightly browned. Add chopped mushrooms and fry for further 5 mins, until cooked. Share mixture between four ramekin dishes.
Mix cream cheese, milk and seasonings together and spread over mushroom mixture. Mix grated cheese and breadcrumbs together and sprinkle over the top. Cook at 190c/375F/Gas 5 for 20-30 mins, until lightly browned and bubbling. Serve hot.
Approx cost £2.50

TIP: Watch out for special offers on mushrooms in your local market. They are often worth buying by the basket if the budget can stretch that far. Wash, cook and freeze in small batches.

WARM CHICKEN LIVER SALAD

8oz/225g frozen chicken livers, defrosted
1/2 head Webb's lettuce
4 Cos lettuce leaves
1/4 cucumber, peeled
2 tbsp oil
4 tbsp dry white wine (or stock)
salt and pepper

METHOD

Separate livers and trim.
Wash lettuces and tear into bite size pieces
and put into a bowl. Cut cucumber in half and
scoop out pips with a teaspoon, cut each half
into thin slices and add to lettuce. Pour half
the oil over and toss lightly. Divide between
four individual plates. Heat the rest of the oil in
a frying pan, add livers and fry over a high heat
for 2-3 mins, until brown, but still tender. Add
wine or stock and seasonings and bring to the
boil. Spoon livers and liquor over salad leaves
and serve immediately.
Approx cost £1.60

SESAME SHRIMP TOASTS

1 200g can shrimps
1/2 tsp salt
1 egg, beaten
3 spring onions, finely chopped
1 tsp ground ginger

1 tbsp soy sauce
4 thin slices bread
2oz/50g sesame seeds
oil for shallow frying

METHOD
Put shrimps into a liquidiser or processor and
whizz until smooth. Add salt, egg onions, ginger and soy and whizz again, until evenly
mixed.
Cut crusts off the bread and spread
each slice with the shrimp paste.
Cut each slice into quarters
and press pasted side into
sesame seeds.
Heat oil and shallow fry,
seeded side first, until
crisp and brown.
Drain on kitchen
paper and serve
hot.
Approx cost £ 2.00

TIP: Use the more expensive fresh or frozen
prawns if you prefer. Health food stalls in the
market are the cheapest place to buy sesame
seeds.

FRITTO MISTO

4oz/100g plain flour
1 egg, beaten
1/2 pint/300ml milk
salt and pepper
oil for deep frying
1/2 small cauliflower, cut into florets
2 courgettes, cut into thick slices
1 potato, cut into cubes
2 carrots, peeled and cut into chunks

METHOD

Put flour, egg and a
little milk into a bowl
and beat well.
Gradually add more
milk, a little at a time

and beating well after each addition, until the
batter is the consistency of double cream (You
may not need all the milk). Season well and
allow to sit for 30 mins.
Heat the oil. Dip the prepared vegetables, a
few at a time, into the batter and drop
carefully into the hot oil. Lift out when browned
all over and drain on kitchen paper. Keep
warm in the oven while the next batch cooks.
Serve hot with a salad garnish.
(Also delicious with cubed fish, prawns,
octopus rings or cubes of hard cheese)
Approx cost £ 2.00

SAVOURY STILTON PUFFS

1/4 pint/150ml water
2oz/50g butter
2 1/2 oz/65g plain flour
1/2 tsp salt
2 eggs, beaten
3oz/75g cream cheese
2oz/50g Stilton cheese
2 tbsp milk
1oz/25g walnuts, chopped

METHOD

Put water and butter in a saucepan and bring
slowly to the boil, to allow the butter to melt.
When the water is boiling tip all the flour and
salt in at once and stir quickly until the mixture
forms a soft ball and leaves the sides of the
pan clean. Allow to cool slightly.
Add eggs, a little at a time, beating well until
the mixture is smooth and shiny, but can still
stand in firm peaks. (You may not need all the
egg.).
Run a baking sheet under cold water. Put walnut-sized spoonfuls of the mixture -spaced well
apart on the damp tray and cook at
200C/400F/Gas 7 for 25-30 mins.
Lift puffs onto a wire rack, after making a
small slit with a knife in the side of each one to
allow the steam to escape, and leave to cool.
Beat the cream cheese, Stilton and milk

together until smooth. Stir in chopped nuts
and use to fill the puffs.
Approx cost £1.80

SPANISH STYLE SLICES

4 thick slices white bread
1 clove garlic, cut in half
4 tbsp olive oil
4 tomatoes, sliced
salt and pepper
8 fresh basil leaves

METHOD

Arrange bread slices on a baking tray and rub
the halved garlic cloves over them. Drizzle a
tablespoon of oil over each one and arrange a
sliced tomato on top. Season well and cook at
190C/375F/Gas 5 for 20-25 mins until
tomatoes are cooked. Roughly chop the basil
leaves and scatter over before serving hot
Approx cost 60p

SMOKED MACKEREL MOUSSE

3 smoked mackerel fillets
¼ pint/ 150ml low fat yogurt
2 tbsp mayonnaise
2 tsp lemon juice
2 spring onions, finely chopped
4 small lettuce leaves
4 thin slices bread

METHOD

Skin fillets and carefully remove any bones. Put fish into a liquidiser or processor and whizz until smooth. Add yogurt, mayonnaise, lemon juice and onions and whizz again, until evenly mixed.

Shred the lettuce and arrange on four individual plates. Put two spoonfuls of the mousse on each plate and add a wedge of lemon.

Toast the bread on both sides. Slip a knife into the side of each slice and cut round to make 8 equal-sized slices. Cut into triangles and toast the untoasted sides. Serve while still warm with the pate.

Approx cost £ 1.50

MELON AND CITRUS STARTER

1 small melon
2 pink grapefruits
4 tbsp oil
1 tbsp white wine vinegar
2 tbsp chopped fresh mint

METHOD

Cut melon in half, remove seeds, cut flesh into bite-size cubes and put into a bowl. Cut the skin off the grapefruit with a sharp knife and use the same knife to cut the flesh from between the membranes, (work over the bowl to catch juice) and add citrus slices to the melon.

Mix oil and vinegar together and pour over fruit. Share between four plates and scatter chopped mint over. Serve chilled.

Approx cost £1.80

TARAMASALATA

1 200g can smoked cod's roe
1 onion, finely chopped or grated
1 clove garlic, crushed
4 slices white bread
5 tbsp milk or water
6 tbsp oil
3 tbsp lemon juice
black pepper

METHOD

Put the roe into a bowl or processor. Add onion and garlic.

Cut the crusts off the bread and leave to soak in the milk or water for 5 mins. Squeeze bread dry and add to the roe mixture. Beat together, or whizz, until smooth. Gradually add the oil and lemon juice and whizz until creamy.

Season well with pepper and chill until required. Serve with warm pitta bread fingers.

Approx cost £1.25

HUMUS

1 439g can cooked chick peas
2oz/50g tahini (sesame seed paste)
4 tbsp lemon juice
4 tbsp olive oil
2 cloves garlic, crushed
black pepper

METHOD

Pour contents of the can into a liquidiser or
processor and whizz until smooth. Add tahini,
lemon juice, oil, garlic and pepper and whizz
again to make a smooth paste. Serve with
warm pitta bread fingers or vegetable crudites.
Approx cost 90p

CRAB PUFFS

1oz/25g butter
2oz/50g mushrooms, finely chopped
1 170g can crabmeat in brine
2 tbsp chopped fresh watercress
1 oz/25g plain flour
¼ pint/150ml milk
1 tbsp sherry(option-
al)
1 tbsp lemon juice
salt and pepper
8oz/225g puff
pastry
1 egg, beaten

METHOD

Melt the butter in a saucepan and fry mush-rooms until tender. Add crab meat and cook for 2-3 mins. Stir in chopped watercress and flour. Remove from heat and gradually add the cream a little at a time, beating well after each addition. Return to the heat and bring to the boil, stirring all the time. Remove from heat, add sherry, lemon juice and seasonings and leave to cool slightly.

Meanwhile roll out the puff pastry to a 16x8 in /40x20cm rectangle and cut into eight 4in/10cm squares.

Put a spoonful of the crab mixture in the cen-tre of each square. Brush the edges with the beaten egg and fold each into a triangle. Press edges together to make a tight seal, knock up the edges and brush with more egg. Arrange on a lightly greased baking sheet and cook at 220c/425F/Gas 7 for 10-15 mins until well risen and brown.

Approx cost £ 2.20

CHICKEN SATAY WITH
PEANUT SAUCE

2 breast chicken, boned, skinned and cut into small cubes
1 tsp chilli powder
5 tbsp water
1 tbsp oil
1 small onion, grated
2 cloves garlic, crushed
2 tbsp lemon juice
4 tbsp crunchy peanut butter
1 tsp salt
1 tsp ground cumin
1 tsp ground coriander

METHOD

Soak 12 wooden bamboo skewers in water for 20 mins (to help prevent burning) before threading three or four chicken cubes on each and cooking under a hot grill until tender. Meanwhile mix chilli powder with 1 tbsp of the water. Heat oil and fry onion, garlic, lemon juice and chilli paste for 5 mins, until onion is soft. Add remaining ingredients and mix together well. Serve hot kebabs with the warm peanut dip and a wedge of lemon.

Approx cost £2.50

COURGETTES A LA GREQUE

4 courgettes, cut into thin slices
salt
4 tbsp olive oil
4 tbsp water
1 tsp ground coriander
salt and freshly ground black pepper
1 tbsp lemon juice
1 397g can chopped tomatoes with herbs
2 cloves garlic, crushed

METHOD

Put courgette slices in a colander, sprinkle
with salt and leave for 30 mins. Rinse and
drain on kitchen paper.
Put all remaining ingredients in a frying pan
and simmer for 5-10 mins. Add courgette
slices and simmer for further 20 mins. Allow
to cool and serve chilled with a crusty roll.
Approx cost £ 1.40

CHEESE CROUSTADES

You"ll need
8 thin slices bread
2oz/50g butter, melted
6oz/175g mushrooms, roughly chopped
4oz/100g soft cheese
1/2 tsp cornflour
2 tbsp chopped fresh parsley
salt and pepper

METHOD

Lightly grease eight holes in a bun tin. Cut the crusts off the bread, flatten slightly with a rolling pin and cut into a round shape. Press one slice into each of the holes. and brush with 1oz/25g of the melted butter. Cook at 200C/400F/Gas 6 for 10-15 mins until crisp and brown.

Add chopped mushrooms to butter remaining in saucepan and cook for 5 mins. Add cheese and stir until melted and mixed together.

Mix cornflour to a smooth paste with a little water and add to mixture. Bring gently to boiling point, stirring all the time. Lower heat, add parsley and seasonings and cook for further 30 secs.

Share mushroom mixture between the bread cases and serve immediately.

Approx cost £1.85

NEOPOLITAN PASTA

8oz/225g dried pasta shapes
1 tbsp oil
1 onion, sliced
2 cloves garlic, crushed
1 397g can chopped tomatoes
1 tsp mixed dried Italian herbs
salt and pepper
2 tbsp grated Parmesan cheese

METHOD

Cook the pasta in lightly salted boiling water until cooked but still 'al dente'. Heat oil and fry onion and garlic until soft. Add canned tomatoes, herbs and seasonings and simmer for 5-10 mins.

Drain pasta and return to pan. Pour sauce over, mix until pasta is evenly coated and divide between four plates. Sprinkle Parmesan cheese over and serve with crusty, or garlic, bread.

Approx cost £ 1.60

TIP: Use grated Cheddar cheese if you don't like Parmesan

EGGS IN CURRY MAYONNAISE

4 eggs, hard boiled
6 tbsp mayonnaise
2 tsp medium curry paste (adjust according to taste)
1 tbsp lemon juice
1 tbsp mango chutney
6 lettuce leaves, shredded
poppadoms

METHOD

Cut the eggs in half and lie two halves, yolk side down, on four individual plates . Mix mayonnaise, curry paste, lemon juice and chutney

together and spoon over the eggs. Serve garnished with the shredded lettuce and poppadoms.
Approx cost £ 1.80

POTATO AND TOMATO STARTER

1lb 450g small new potatoes, scrubbed and cooked
4 eggs, hardboiled
8 small lettuce leaves
2 tomatoes, cut into thin wedges
2 tbsp oil
1 tbsp white wine vinegar
1/2 tsp coarse grain mustard
salt and pepper

METHOD

Leave the potatoes whole if possible, or cut into bite-size pieces and keep warm.
Shell eggs and slice them. Share the lettuce leaves between four individual plates, and arrange the potatoes, eggs and tomatoes on top.
Mix oil, vinegar, mustard and seasonings together and drizzle dressing over the salad.
Serve immediately, while the potatoes are still warm.
Approx cost £ 1.25

POTTED SMOKED MACKEREL

2 smoked mackerel fillets
1/2 oz/15g butter
1/2 oz/15g plain flour
1/2 pint/300ml milk
2oz/50g grated cheese
1 tsp mustard powder
salt and pepper

METHOD

Remove skin and any bones from fish before
flaking into small pieces.
Melt butter in a saucepan, add flour and cook
gently for 1 min. Remove from heat and gradually add milk a little at a time, beating well after
each addition. Return to the heat and bring
gently to the boil, stirring all the time.
Remove from heat and add half the grated
cheese and seasonings. Stir in the flaked fish
and divide the mixture between four ramekin
dishes. Top with remaining grated cheese and
pop under a hot grill until it is melted, browned
and bubbling. Serve immediately.

Approx cost £ 1.60

CHAPTER THREE
LETT-UCE EAT

Salads mean 'rabbit food' to a lot of people but they needn't be a mixture of lettuce cucumber and tomato.

There is a huge selection of leaves to choose from now, although some of the posh lettuces are expensive. (It's easy to plant some seeds and grow your own if you have the space.) Choose from Cos Webbs, Little gem, Lollo rosso, Iceberg, Oak leaf and round lettuces. Add a mixture of other leaves to make a green salad try spinach, dandelion leaves, watercress, chinese leaves or salad cress.

Break leaves off, wash, shake or spin dry (in a salad spinner) and store in a poly bag in the fridge. Tear leaves into bite-size pieces rather than cut them as they won't brown so quickly.

Add shredded white cabbage cucumber, spring onions, green peppers or celery to make a simple salad.

SHOOTING AHEAD

Sprout your own beans and add extra crunch and fibre to salads. Try mung, aduki, alfalfa or black-eyed beans. Rinse well and discard the grotty ones. Fill a jam jar one quarter full with beans, fill with water, cover and leave overnight. Drain and rinse again the next day, but pour off excess water. Lie jar on its side and cover with a tea towel to keep dark. Rinse beans every day and use when 1 ^{1}/2in/4cm long - 3-6days, depending on size.

Eat raw in salads or add to stir fries.

SALAD DRESSINGS

Use sunflower or rape seed oil, or olive or nut-flavoured oils if you prefer, although they are more expensive. Make your own seasoned oils by putting crushed garlic or the herbs into a bottle and allowing the flavour to develop. White or red wine vinegar are best for salads as malt vinegar is too heavy and the flavour too strong. Herb, fruit or garlic flavoured vinegars can easily be made at home and add extra tang to the salad.

BASIC VINAIGRETTE DRESSING

8 tbsp oil
2 tbsp vinegar
1 tsp coarse grain mustard
salt and pepper

Put all ingredients in a screw top jar and shake well. Store in the fridge.

VARIATIONS

Add 1 crushed clove garlic or 2 tsp mixed dried herbs to the dressing. Or add 2 tbsp lemon juice instead of the vinegar.

MAYONNAISE

2 egg yolks (at room temperature)
1 tsp vinegar
1/2 tsp mustard powder
1/4pint/ 150ml oil
salt and pepper

METHOD

Put egg yolks, mustard and $1/2$ tsp vinegar in a bowl or liquidiser. Whisk or whizz and add oil, a few drops at a time, mixing all the time. Gradually add oil in a thin trickle until mixture is thick and creamy. Season well. If the oil is added too fast or the egg are too cold the mixture will curdle and look like scrambled eggs.

Whisk in 1 tbsp boiling water and if that fails, break another egg yolk into a clean bowl or liquidise and slowly add curdled mixture, beating all the time. You will have to add another 3-4 tbsp oil as well.

Variations

Add crushed garlic cloves, chopped fresh herbs, lemon juice or 1 tbsp tomato puree to the finished mayonnaise. Of course you could always buy mayonnaise or salad cream, if you prefer, from the supermarket.

Most recipes make a main course salad but there are some side or smaller salads amongst them. Adjust amounts for larger or smaller numbers.

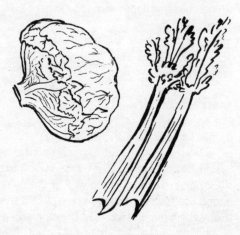

SALADS

SALAD NICOISE

8oz/225g French beans, topped and tailed
1 197g can tuna in brine
8oz/225g tomatoes, cut into thin wedges
1 small onion, thinly sliced
2oz/50g black olives(optional)
6 Cos lettuce leaves
4 tbsp oil
1 tbsp white wine vinegar
1/2 tsp coarse grain mustard
3 eggs, hard boiled
salt and pepper

METHOD

Steam the beans in a colander over a pan of boiling water for 5 mins, until tender but not soft. Rinse under cold water and leave to drain.
Flake the tuna and remove any bones and put into a bowl with the tomatoes, onion and olives.
Tear the lettuce into bite-size pieces and add to the bowl with the beans
Mix the oil, vinegar, mustard and seasonings together and pour over the salad before carefully stirring in the eggs. Serve with fresh bread.
Approx cost £ 2.50

WARM SPINACH SALAD

1lb/450g potatoes, scrubbed
6 rashers rindless streaky bacon
12oz/350g spinach leaves, washed
4 tbsp oil
2 tbsp white wine vinegar
1 tsp coarse grain mustard
salt and pepper

METHOD

Cut the potatoes into large cubes and cook in
lightly salted boiling water until tender. Drain
and keep warm.
Grill bacon until crisp and cut into small pieces.
Rinse spinach and spin, or shake, dry.
Mix oil, vinegar, mustard and seasonings
together in a large bowl. Add warm potatoes
and stir well. Add spinach and bacon, toss
together and serve immediately
Approx cost £ 1.50

GREEK SALAD

1 crisp lettuce, washed
2oz/50g white cabbage, finely shredded
3 large tomatoes, cut into wedges
¼ cucumber, sliced
1 small onion, sliced
2oz/50g black olives
2oz/50g Feta cheese
3 tbsp olive oil

1 tbsp lemon juice
2 sprigs chopped fresh mint
salt and pepper

METHOD

Tear the lettuce into bite-size pieces and put in
a large bowl. Add shredded cabbage, tomatoes, cucumber, sliced onion and olives. Mix
well. Cut the Feta cheese into cubes and stir
into salad.
Mix the oil, lemon juice, mint and seasonings
together and pour over salad. Toss well and
serve with warm pitta bread

Approx cost £ 2.00

TIP: Olives can be expensive but make all the
difference to a salad. They usually come in
brine but keep, and taste, better if you pour it
off and fill with oil instead.

BROWN RICE SALAD

12oz/350g brown rice
2 courgettes, chopped
2 sticks celery, chopped
1 red pepper, de-seeded and chopped
2 spring onions, chopped
2 tomatoes, chopped
4 tbsp oil
1 tbsp lemon juice
1 clove garlic, crushed
salt and pepper

METHOD

Cook the rice according to pack instructions, about 30-35 mins, rinse and drain. Turn into a bowl. Add courgettes, celery,pepper, spring onions and tomatoes.

Mix the oil, lemon juice, garlic and seasonings together and pour over salad. Toss well and serve with granary rolls.

Approx cost £ 1.75

CHICKEN AND APRICOT SALAD

1 tbsp oil
1 onion, finely chopped
2 chicken breasts, cut into thin strips
1 tbsp curry paste
1 tsp ground coriander
2 tbsp lemon juice
¼ pint/150ml mayonnaise
¼ pint/150ml natural yogurt
4oz/100g dried ready-to-eat apricots
salt and pepper
1 small crisp lettuce, washed
1 tbsp dessicated coconut, toasted

METHOD

Heat oil and fry onion until softened. Add chicken strips, curry paste and coriander and fry gently for 4-5 mins until cooked. Add lemon juice and leave to cool.

Put mayonnaise and yogurt into a bowl and mix

well. Add onion mixture, apricots, and seasonings and stir to coat evenly.

Arrange lettuce leaves on a platter and pile chicken salad on top. Scatter the toasted coconut over the top and serve.

Approx cost £3.25

TIP: thinly slice drained, canned apricots to save more money.

BACON AND POTATO SALAD

1 1/2lb/675g waxy potatoes, scrubbed and cut into slices
8oz/225g rindless streaky bacon, chopped
1 onion, chopped
4 tbsp white wine vinegar
4 tbsp water
3 spring onions, chopped
2 tbsp chopped fresh parsley

METHOD

Cook the potatoes in lightly salted boiling water for 10 mins, until just tender.

Fry the bacon and onion in a frying pan until crisp Add vinegar, water and spring onions and simmer for 5 mins. Drain potatoes add to bacon mixture and stir well. Sprinkle with chopped parsley and serve immediately.

Approx cost £1.60

WALDORF SALAD

3 cox's apples, quartered, cored and sliced
2 tbsp lemon juice
4 sticks celery, sliced
2oz/50g walnuts, chopped
4 tbsp mayonnaise
3 tbsp natural yogurt
salt and pepper
1 crisp lettuce

METHOD

Put the sliced apple immediately into the lemon
juice to prevent browning. Add celery and walnuts and mix well. Mix the mayonnaise, natural
yogurt and seasonings together and add to
salad. Toss together lightly. Line a salad bowl
with the lettuce leaves and pile salad in the
centre. Serve immediately with brown baps.
Approx cost £ 1.70

CAESER SALAD

2 cloves garlic
1/4 pint/150ml oil
2 thick slices bread
1/2 Cos lettuce
4 eggs
2 tbsp olive oil
2 tsp lemon juice
1/4 tsp Tabasco sauce
2 tbsp grated Parmesan cheese

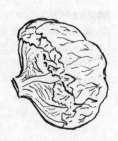

METHOD

Peel the garlic and wipe round the salad bowl
before crushing.

Heat oil in a frying pan. Cut crusts off the
bread and cut into small cubes and shallow fry
them a few at a time in the hot oil, until very
crisp. Drain on kitchen paper.

Tear the lettuce leaves into bite-size pieces and
put in the salad bowl. Boil the eggs for 4-5
mins, rinse with cold water and shell.

Mix, olive oil, juice, garlic, Tabasco and
Parmesan cheese together.

Pour the dressing over the leaves and toss
well. Add croutons and divide salad between
four plates. Top with an egg each and serve.

Approx cost £ 1.40

PASTA TUNA SALAD

12oz/350g dried pasta shapes
1 197g can tuna in oil
3 spring onions, finely chopped
1/2 cucumber, roughly chopped
6 tbsp mayonnaise
2 tbsp natural yogurt
grated rind and juice of 1 lemon
salt and pepper
1/2 crisp lettuce

METHOD

Cook the pasta in lightly salted boiling water.
Rinse with cold water and leave to drain. Turn
into a large bowl. Flake tuna and add to pasta
with the oil. Add onions and cucumber and
toss together. Mix mayonnaise, yogurt, lemon
rind and juice and seasonings together and stir
into salad until evenly coated. Shred lettuce
and arrange round the edge of a platter. Pile
tuna and pasta in the centre and serve.
Approx cost £2.10

MIXED MOROCCAN SALAD

1 1/2 lb/675g waxy potatoes, cooked and
diced
2 carrots, peeled, diced and cooked
1 green pepper, de-seeded and chopped
3 tomatoes, roughly chopped
2oz/50g black olives
4 tbsp olive oil
2 tbsp lemon juice
1 tbsp chopped fresh parsley
1 tsp ground coriander

METHOD

Put the cooked, diced vegetables in a bowl
together. Add pepper, tomatoes and olives and
toss together.
Mix oil, lemon juice, parsley and coriander
together and pour over salad. Toss together

until evenly coated and mixed and chill before
serving with crusty bread.
Approx cost £ 1.80

CRACKED WHEAT SALAD

8oz/225g cracked wheat or bulgur
1 orange pepper, de-seeded and diced
2 tomatoes, chopped
1/4 cucumber, chopped
2 sticks celery, chopped
4oz/100g smoked pork sausage, sliced
2 tbsp oil
1 tbsp lemon juice
salt and pepper
2 tbsp chopped fresh mint

METHOD

Put the cracked wheat in a large bowl and
cover with boiling water. Leave to swell and
cook, topping up with more water if necessary.
Drain any excess water off before adding
chopped pepper, tomatoes, cucumber, celery
and pork sausage and mix well.
Mix oil, juice, seasonings and fresh mint
together and pour over the salad. Toss well
and serve.
Approx cost £1.90

CHINESE STYLE SALAD

4 eggs, beaten
salt and pepper
2 tbsp oil
1 tbsp soy sauce
1 tsp ground ginger
4oz/100g mushrooms, quartered
2 carrots, peeled and cut into thin matchsticks
4 spring onions, chopped
4oz/100g fresh beansprouts
4 Chinese leaves, shredded

METHOD

Mix eggs with a little water and beat well. Add seasonings. Heat a little oil in a small frying pan, pour a quarter of the mixture in and cook until set. Turn out, roll up and keep warm. Repeat with the remaining mixture to make 4 small rolled-up omelettes.

Meanwhile put the oil and soy in a bowl, add ginger and mushrooms, carrots and spring onions and leave to marinate for 20-30 mins. Add beansprouts and Chinese leaves and stir well. Share between four plates.

Thinly slice the omelettes and arrange over the top of the salads.

Approx cost £1.90

MACKEREL AND CUCUMBER SALAD

1 cucumber
1 small onion, thinly sliced
4 tbsp white wine vinegar
1 tsp sugar
1 crisp lettuce
2 tbsp oil
3 smoked peppered mackerel fillets

METHOD

Cut cucumber in half lengthways and scoop out the seeds with a teaspoon. Cut into very thin slices. Put into a bowl with onion, vinegar and sugar and leave to marinate for 30 mins. Tear lettuce into bite-size pieces and add to the salad with the oil. Toss together. Skin the mackerel, remove any bones and flake into the salad. Toss well and serve with crusty brown bread.

Approx cost £1.90

EASTERN SALAD

1 head celeriac, peeled and cut into thin matchsticks
3 tbsp lemon juice
1 head chicory, finely shredded
2oz/50g mangetout, lihtly cooked
4oz/100g beansprouts
2 eggs, hard boiled

4 tbsp oil
1 tbsp white wine vinegar
1 tsp mustard
juice of half an orange
salt and pepper

METHOD
Put celeriac in a bowl, and toss in lemon juice.
Add shredded chicory, mangetout, and
beansprouts and stir well.
Shell eggs, cut in half and lift out yolks. Finely
chop both.
Mix oil, vinegar, mustard, juice and seasonings
together, add chopped egg and pour over
salad. Toss well and serve.
Approx cost £2.00

CHEF'S SALAD
1 round lettuce, washed
1 head radicchio, washed
1 green pepper, de-seeded and diced
2 sticks celery, chopped
2 red apples, quartered, cored and diced
1oz sultanas
2 tbsp mayonnaise
3 tbsp single cream or natural yogurt
1 tsp lemon juice
4oz/100g cooked ham, diced
4oz/100g cheese, cubed

METHOD

Tear the salad leaves into bite-size pieces and put in a bowl. Add pepper, celery, apples and sultanas.

Stir together the mayonnaise, single cream and lemon juice and add to salad, stir until evenly coated. Add chopped ham and cheese and stir again. Serve with warm bread.

Approx cost £2.75

SPICY RICE SALAD

12oz/350g basmati rice
1 tsp salt
2 tsp Madras curry powder
4 tbsp oil
4 tomatoes, chopped
1 227g can pineapple pieces
2oz/50g sultanas
1 tbsp sherry (optional)
1 tsp ground cumin
1 tsp ground coriander

METHOD

Put rice, 1 pint/600ml water, salt and curry powder in a saucepan and bring to the boil. Reduce heat and simmer for 8-10 mins, until cooked. Add 1 tbsp oil, tomatoes, pineapple and a little juice and sultanas, and stir well.

Mix remaining oil, sherry, cumin and coriander together and pour over salad. Toss well and serve slightly warm with bread or poppadoms.
Approx cost £2.20

BLUE CHEESE SLAW

3 red skinned apples, quartered, cored and diced
1 tbsp lemon juice
12oz/350g red cabbage, finely shredded
3 sticks celery, thinly sliced
2oz/50g hazelnuts, toasted
2oz/50g soft blue cheese
4 tbsp mayonnaise
4 tbsp milk
salt and pepper

METHOD

Toss the diced apple in the lemon juice, to prevent discolouration, in a bowl. Add cabbage, celery and toasted nuts and stir. Beat the blue cheese, mayonnaise, milk and seasonings together and add to salad. Toss vegetables gently until evenly coated and serve with fresh bread.
Approx cost £2.20

CURRIED BEAN SALAD

4 tomatoes
1oz/25g butter

2 tbsp oil
1 onion, thinly sliced
2 cloves garlic, crushed
1 439g can chick peas
1 415g can red kidney beans
1 435g can butter beans
1/4 pint/150ml natural yogurt
2 tsp mild or medium curry
paste, according to taste
2 tsp ground coriander

METHOD

Put the tomatoes in a bowl and pour boiling water over. Leave for 15 mins before peeling off skins and roughly chopping.

Put butter and oil in a saucepan and fry onion and garlic for 5 mins, until soft but not brown. Add chopped tomatoes.

Drain and rinse all the beans and add to tomato mixture. Cook for 5-10 mins before turning into a salad bowl.

Mix yogurt, curry paste and coriander together before stirring into the bean mixture. Serve warm.

Approx cost £2.20

TIP: Use canned chopped tomatoes instead of fresh ones if they work out cheaper.

FENNEL AND TOMATO SALAD

1 large bulb fennel
1 onion, thinly sliced
4 tomatoes, cut into thin wedges
¼ cucumber
2 apples, quartered, cored and sliced
2 tbsp lemon juice
3 tbsp oil
salt and pepper

METHOD

Trim fennel and cut into thin slices. Drop into
lightly salted boiling water for 2 mins, drain
and cold rinse. Transfer to salad bowl. Add
onion and tomatoes. Cut cucumber in half
lengthways and scoop out seeds. Cut into thin
slices and add to fennel. Toss the sliced apples
in the lemon juice and add to salad. Drizzle oil
over and season. Toss together and serve with
granary bread

Approx cost £1.80

CHICK PEA SALAD

1 439g can cooked chick peas
8oz/225g French beans, topped and tailed
5 tbsp mayonnaise
2 tbsp natural yogurt
2 cloves garlic, crushed
1 50g tin anchovy fillets, drained and chopped
3 spring onions, finely chopped

2 tbsp chopped fresh parsley
1 tbsp lemon juice
salt and pepper
1/2 lettuce
2oz/50g black olives

METHOD

Drain and rinse chick peas and put into a salad
bowl. Steam the French beans in a colander
over boiling water for 2-3 mins, cold rinse, cut
in half and add to the chick peas.

Mix the mayonnaise with the yogurt and
crushed garlic. Add anchovies, onions, parsley
lemon juice and seasonings. Mix with the chick
peas and beans and leave to stand for 20
mins.

Arrange the lettuce leaves on plates and top
with the salad. Scatter the olives over and
serve.

Approx cost £2.60

CHUNKY VEGETABLE SALAD

1/2 small white cabbage, shredded
1/2 small red cabbage, shredded
2 carrots, peeled and grated
1 small cauliflower cut into florets
1/2 cucumber. chopped
4 tomatoes, chopped
2oz/50g mushrooms, chopped
4 tbsp oil
1 tbsp vinegar
2oz/50g salted peanuts
4oz/100g Edam cheese, grated
4oz/100g Red Leicester cheese, grated

METHOD

Put the shredded cabbage in a large bowl with
the carrots, cauliflower, cucumber, tomatoes
and mushrooms. Mix together.
In a small bowl mix the oil and vinegar together
and pour over salad. Toss well. Add peanuts
and stir again.
Serve with a mixture of grated cheeses and
sliced wholemeal bread.
Approx cost £ 3.00

AVOCADO SALAD

8 rashers rindless streaky bacon
6 Cos lettuce leaves, shredded
3 tbsp olive oil
1 tbsp white wine vinegar

salt and pepper
1/2 tsp coarse grain mustard
2 avocados

METHOD

Grill bacon until crisp and snip into small
pieces.
Arrange shredded lettuce on four plates. Mix
the oil, vinegar and mustard together in a
bowl. Peel, stone and slice the two avocados
and place on plates with lettuce. Drizzle dressing over, scatter the crispy bacon over the top.
Serve with granary rolls.
Approx cost £ 1.80

HOT POTATO AND TUNA

12oz/350g new potatoes, scrubbed
5 tbsp olive oil
1 onion, sliced
1 200g can tuna in oil
1 red pepper, de-seeded and chopped
1 tbsp white wine vinegar
1 tsp coarse grain mustard
salt and pepper
1 crisp lettuce

METHOD

Cook the potatoes in lightly salted boiling water
until tender.
Meanwhile heat oil in a frying pan and fry onion

until softened. Drain and flake the tuna, discarding any bones and add to the pan. Add red pepper, white wine vinegar, mustard and seasonings. Simmer gently for 2-3 mins, until warmed through.

Drain the potatoes and turn into a salad bowl. Pour the contents of the frying pan over and toss gently.

Shred lettuce and arrange on plates to serve with hot salad.

Approx cost £2.20

BEANSPROUT SALAD

8oz/225g beansprouts, or mixed sprouted beans
1 small iceberg lettuce, shredded
4 cabbage leaves finely shredded
5 tbsp oil
1 tbsp lemon juice
salt and pepper
2 spring onions, finely chopped

METHOD

Pick out any unsprouted beans and rinse the rest well with cold water. Drain and put into a salad bowl. Add shredded leaves and toss together.

Mix the oil, lemon juice and seasonings together and pour over the salad.

Toss well and scatter spring onions over the top. Serve immediately.
Approx cost £2.40

CURRIED VEGETABLE SALAD

2 tbsp oil
1 onion, chopped
2 cloves garlic, crushed
2 tsp ground ginger
2 tsp medium curry powder, according to taste
3 carrots, peeled and thinly sliced
1 cauliflower, cut into florets
salt and pepper
4oz/100g green beans, topped and tailed

METHOD

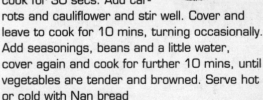

Heat oil and fry onion and garlic until lightly browned. Add ginger and curry powder and cook for 30 secs. Add carrots and cauliflower and stir well. Cover and leave to cook for 10 mins, turning occasionally. Add seasonings, beans and a little water, cover again and cook for further 10 mins, until vegetables are tender and browned. Serve hot or cold with Nan bread
Approx cost £1.50

TOMATO RICE

12oz/350g long grain rice
1 397g can chopped tomatoes with herbs
2 tbsp oil
1 onion, chopped
2 cloves garlic, crushed
4oz/100g mushrooms, sliced
1 tbsp red wine vinegar
salt and pepper

METHOD

After rinsing the rice put it in a saucepan with the canned tomatoes and one can of water. Season well and bring to the boil. Simmer for 10-12 mins, until the rice is tender.
Heat oil and fry onion and garlic until starting to brown, add mushrooms and cook for 5 mins, until mushrooms soften. Add red wine vinegar, adjust seasoning and pour over rice. Serve hot or cold.

Approx cost £1.50

COLESLAW

1 small white cabbage, finely shredded
1 small onion, finely sliced
2 sticks celery, thinly sliced
3 carrots, peeled and grated
2oz/50g sultanas
4 tbsp mayonnaise
2 tbsp natural yogurt
salt and pepper

METHOD

Put the shredded cabbage in a large bowl and add onion, celery, carrots and sultanas. Toss together.
Mix the mayonnaise, yogurt and seasonings together and stir into vegetables, until evenly coated. Leave for one hour before serving with jacket potatoes.

Approx cost £1.30

RED SLAW

2 large oranges
1 small red cabbage, finely shredded
4 tbsp mayonnaise
2 tbsp natural yogurt
salt and pepper

METHOD

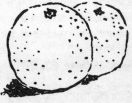

Cut the skin off the oranges with a serrated knife. Hold over the salad bowl and cut segments between membranes. Put into the salad with the shredded cabbage.
Mix mayonnaise and yogurt together, season well and stir into cabbage until evenly coated.

Approx cost £1.10

HOT SPICY POTATO SALAD

1lb/450g sweet potatoes, scrubbed
1 small cauliflower, cut into florets
2oz/50g butter
1 orange pepper, de-seeded and sliced
1 340g can sweetcorn, drained and rinsed
2 tsp ground cumin
1 tsp chilli powder, according to taste
salt and pepper

METHOD

Cook the potatoes whole in lightly salted boiling
water for 15 mins, or until tender. Steam the
cauliflower florets in a colander over the potatoes for the last five minutes of cooking time.
Drain potatoes and cut into thick slices.
Melt butter in a frying pan and add cauliflower,
potatoes, pepper and sweetcorn. Fry for 2-3
mins before adding cumin and chilli powder.
Season well and cook for further 3 mins before
serving hot.

Approx cost £2.20

SMOKED TROUT SALAD

1 smoked trout
bunch radishes, sliced
4 sticks celery, thinly sliced
3 eggs, hard boiled, roughly chopped
1/2 cucumber, sliced
1 bunch watercress, washed and stalks
removed

4oz/100g peeled prawns
5 tbsp mayonnaise
1 tbsp white wine vinegar
2 tbsp milk
2 tsp coarse grain mustard
1 tsp horseradish sauce

METHOD

Bone fish carefully - run a knife along the backbone and peel skin off one side. Lift fillets off
and flake fish.

Put radishes, celery, eggs, cucumber, watercress and prawns in a bowl. Add fish and stir
gently.

Mix mayonnaise with the vinegar, milk, mustard and horseradish and add to salad. Stir
gently until evenly coated and serve.

Approx cost £3.50

TIP: Save this one for a treat! Or swap the
trout for tuna, and the fresh prawns for the
tinned type.

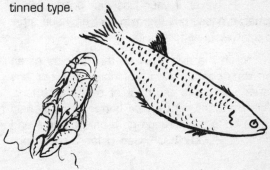

CHAPTER FOUR

THE MAIN CHANCE

DINNER JACKETS

Choose old potatoes that are roughly the same size so they are cooked at the same time. However if your kids can only manage smaller ones, put them in half an hour after the larger ones for adults.

Scrub the skins well so they can be eaten as they contain plenty of fibre. Cut out any 'eyes' and stalks and prick all over with a fork. Rub the skins with a little butter or oil to help them crisp up, arrange on a baking sheet and cook at 200C/400F/Gas 6 for 3/4-1 hour for small spuds and 1-1$^1/_2$ hours for larger ones. Check by piercing with a knife to see if they are tender.

It is possible to cut down the baking time by putting in a pan of cold water and bringing to the boil before transferring to the oven, or part-cooking them in a microwave.

Although they are delicious when served as a vegetable accompaniment, they are also an excellent filling meal in themselves. Try them topped with a knob of butter and grated cheese, cottage cheese with chives or fruit, sausages and beans or canned stews.

When the potatoes are cooked remove from the oven and cut a cross in the top. Squeeze the sides to loosen potato and top with filling.

Here's five fabulous fillings for the family to choose from;

All recipes are to serve four.

TIP: Supermarkets kindly pick out, wash and pre-pack baking potatoes but they can work out much more expensive. Rummage through the self-selection and choose your own - they'll probably be cheaper.

CHILLI JACKETS

1 tbsp oil
1 onion, chopped
2 cloves garlic, crushed
8oz/225g beef mince
1 397g can chopped tomatoes with herbs
1 tbsp tomato puree
2 tsp chilli powder, according to taste
salt and pepper
1 220g can kidney beans

METHOD

Heat oil and fry onion and garlic until starting to brown. Add mince and fry until browned all over. Add chopped tomatoes, puree, chilli powder, seasonings and a little water and leave to simmer for 30-45 mins, until thickened. Drain and rinse kidney beans before adding to the mince and cooking for further 15 mins, until heated through.
Serve hot
Approx cost £1.40

BACON AND EGG

1 tbsp oil
1 onion, sliced
8 rashers rindless
streaky bacon
4 eggs

METHOD

Heat oil in a pan and fry onions until browned. Grill bacon until crisp and drain on kitchen paper. Push onions to one side of the pan and fry the eggs. Put a spoonful of onion, two rashers of bacon and one egg in each potato.

Approx cost £1.10

TUNA AND SWEETCORN

1oz/25g butter or margarine
1 onion, finely chopped
1oz/25g plain flour
1/2 pint/300ml milk
1 200g/7oz can tuna in brine, drained and flaked
1 198g can sweetcorn, drained
salt and pepper

METHOD

Melt the butter in a saucepan and fry onions until softened. Stir in flour and cook for 30 secs. Remove from heat and gradually add the milk, a little at a time and beat well after each addition. Return to the heat and bring to the boil, stirring all the time until thickened. Add tuna, sweetcorn and seasonings and simmer for 2 mins, before serving.

Approx cost £1.30

QUICK CHICKEN CURRY

1 tbsp oil
1 onion, finely chopped
2 cloves garlic, crushed
1 chicken breast, finely sliced
1 397g can chopped tomatoes
2 tsp Madras curry powder, according to taste
salt and pepper
4 tbsp natural yogurt

METHOD

Heat oil and fry onion and garlic until browned.
Add sliced chicken and fry until cooked and
firm. Add chopped tomatoes, curry powder
and seasonings. Cover and simmer for 30-40
mins, until cooked and thickened. Stir in natural yogurt, heat gently and serve.
Approx cost £1.40

HOT DOGS

1 113g can hot dog sausages, drained and
chopped
1 198g can sweeetcorn, drained
2 tbsp milk
salt and pepper
2oz/50g cheese, grated

METHOD

Scoop the potato out of the skins and put in a
bowl. Add the chopped hot dogs, sweetcorn,

milk and seasonings and mix together. Put the
mixture back into the skins and level the tops.
Scatter cheese over and put back in the oven
for 15-20 mins, until browned and bubbling.
Approx cost £1.10

QUICHES

The quiche has become very popular and is even available by the slice at most deli counters in supermarkets, but they are incredibly cheap and easy to make, depending on your filling.

There are three simple rules to guarantee a successful quiche and abolish soggy bottoms!

1. Use a metal flan case and sit it on a metal baking sheet as this conducts the heat better to help crisp up the base.

2. Always bake the pastry case 'blind' (empty) before putting in the filling to give the pastry a chance to set and crisp up.

3. Let the pastry case rest for 10 mins before putting the filling in, brush with a beaten egg if you can run to it to seal the pastry.

SOUPS (Listed clockwise from top)
Carrot and Coriander, Pasta and vegetable.
Tomato and Basil, Beetroot and Apple, Chilli Bean.
Vegetable and Bread and French Onion.

STARTERS *(Listed clockwise from top)*
Lettuce Wrap, Felafels and Cucumber Raita
Individual Leek Flan, Hummus, Taramasalata,
Potato skins and Vegetable crudites, Chicken
Satay with Peanut sauce.

SALADS (Listed clockwise from top)
Chicken and Apricot Salad, Greek Salad, Chinese
Salad, Salad Nicoise, Spicy Rice, Salad,
Avocado Salad.

MAIN MEALS - MEAT *(Listed clockwise from top)*
Bacon and Leek Roly Poly, Chicken Crisp, Chicken
Parcels, Spicy Chicken Drumsticks, Sausage and
onion Toad, Meat balls in Barbecue Sauce

MAIN MEALS - VEGGIE (Listed clockwise from top) Potato Pie, Spicy Bean Pie, Nutty Fritters, Spanish Totilla, Pasta Pesto Cheesey Aubergine Bake

HOT DESSERTS (Listed clockwise from top)
Sweet Batter Pudding, Chocolate Bread and
Butter Pudding, Treacle Tarts, Peach Upside
Down Pud, Apple and Mincemeat Roll. Gooseberry
and Apple Meringues

COLD DESSERTS (Listed clockwise from top)Profiteroles and Chocolate sauce, Raspberry Mousse, Fruity Meringue, Creme Caramel, Toute Suite Trifle, Portuguese Orange Roll, Apricot Creams.

SNACKS *(listed clockwise from top)*
Pate Parcels, Sausage stuffed Pittas, Mini-Quiches, Red Flannel Hash, Eggs Provencale.

If making pastry isn't your strong point, short-crust and wholemeal should be available, fresh or frozen, from most supermarkets.

Use the recipe for pastry for all quiches and choose one of the fillings

SHORTCRUST PASTRY

To line an 8in/20cm shallow flan tin
6oz/175g plain flour
3oz/75g butter or margarine
1/4 tsp salt
cold water to mix

METHOD

Put flour into a bowl. Cut butter or marg into small pieces and add salt. Use fingertips to rub the fat into the flour, until mixture resembles fine breadcrumbs; Add enough cold water, a little at a time to knead into a firm dough. Keep hands cold and handle the mixture for as short a time as possible to keep the pastry light.

Put into as poly bag and chill for 20 mins.

Turn onto a lightly floured surface and knead gently. Roll out until large enough to line the flan tin.

Press firmly into place and prick the base all over with a fork. Put back in the fridge for 10 mins. Cook at 180C/375F/Gas 4 for 15 mins. Remove from oven and brush with beaten egg and return to the oven for further

5 mins. Remove from oven and allow to cool for 10 mins before filling.

Once the filling is in return to the oven for further 30-40 mins, until set and browned.

Roll out and cook bought shortcrust or wholemeal pastry in the same way.

Each quiche should cut into eight slices

ONION TART

1 tbsp oil
4 large onions, cut into rings
3 eggs, beaten
1/2 pint/150ml milk
salt and pepper
2oz/50g cheese, grated

METHOD

Heat the oil and fry the onions until starting to brown.

Beat the eggs, milk and seasonings together and pour half into the pastry case. Scatter the onion rings. Pour remaining egg mixture over and scatter cheese over the top. Lift carefully into the oven and cook as before.

Serve hot or cold

Approx cost £1.50

POTATO AND BACON

1lb/450g potatoes, diced
1 tbsp oil

8oz/225g rindless streaky bacon
1 onion, sliced
1 clove garlic, crushed
3 eggs, beaten
1/2 pint/300ml milk
salt and pepper

METHOD

Boil potatoes in lightly salted water for 10
mins, or until tender and drain. Heat oil and fry
bacon, onion and garlic until lightly browned.
Lift out of pan onto a plate. Fry cooked potatoes in pan for 5 mins, until lightly browned.
Return bacon mixture to pan and and stir gently together. Transfer to cooled pastry case.
Beat eggs, milk and seasoning together and
pour over potato mixture. Lift carefully into the
oven and cook until set and browned.
Approx cost £1.50

MUSHROOM AND SALAMI

1 tbsp oil
1 onion, thinly sliced
8oz/225g mushrooms, sliced
2 courgettes, thinly sliced
4oz/100g salami, snipped into strips
3 eggs, beaten
1/2 pint/300ml milk
salt and pepper
2oz/50g cheese, grated

METHOD

Heat oil and fry onion until softened, add sliced mushrooms and courgettes and fry for further 8 - 10 mins, until vegetables are tender.

Arrange in cooled flan case. Scatter strips of salami over the top.

Beat eggs, milk and seasoning together and pour over vegetables. Scatter grated cheese over and lift carefully into the oven. Cook until set, golden browned and bubbling

Approx cost £2.50

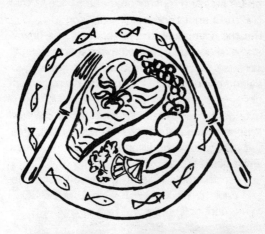

MAIN MEALS

BACON AND MUSHROOM ROLL

12oz/350g rindless streaky bacon, chopped
2 onions, chopped
2 tsp dried mixed herbs
8oz/225g mushrooms, thinly sliced
10oz/300g plain flour
5oz/150g suet
salt and pepper
1 beaten egg, or milk, to glaze

METHOD

Put bacon, onions and herbs into a frying pan
and fry for 10-12 mins, until starting to brown

and crisp. Add mushrooms and fry for further 5-8 mins until cooked.

Put the flour, suet and seasonings in a bowl and add enough water to make a firm dough. Turn onto a lightly floured surface, knead gently and roll out to a 10x8in/25x20cm rectangle.

Put the bacon filling along one half of the pastry and brush the edges with egg or milk. Fold the pastry over the filling and pinch the edges well to seal tightly.

Lift carefully onto a lightly greased baking sheet and cook at 180C/375F/Gas 4 for 20-30 mins, until golden brown. Serve hot.

Approx cost £2.50

PASTA AND BEAN BAKE

8oz/225g dried pasta shapes
1 small cauliflower, cut into florets
1 tbsp oil
3 courgettes, sliced
2 440g cans spicy mixed beans
1 397g can chopped tomatoes with herbs
8oz/225g fresh breadcrumbs
1 tbsp dried mixed herbs
4oz/100g cheese, grated

METHOD

Cook the pasta in lightly salted boiling water, approx 12 mins, and drain. Steam the cauli-

flower in a colander, over the boiling water for
8-10 mins, until tender.
Heat the oil and fry the courgettes until brown.
Mix the pasta, cauliflower, courgettes, beans
and tomatoes together and transfer to an
ovenproof dish.
Mix the breadcrumbs with herbs and half the
grated cheese and sprinkle over the bean mixture. Scatter remaining cheese over, press
down well and cook at 190C/375F/Gas 5 for
30-40 mins, until golden brown. Serve hot
Approx cost £2.75

TIP: Save fuel by steaming vegetables in a
colander, or steamer, over the boiling potatoes.

SAUSAGE AND ONION TOAD
1lb/450g fresh sausages
1 onion, sliced
4oz/100g plain flour
1/2 tsp salt
2 eggs, beaten
1/2 pint/300ml milk
1 tsp dried mixed herbs

METHOD
Arrange sausages in a 3 1/2 pint/1.7litre
roasting tin and scatter sliced onions over. Put
into a hot oven and cook at 220C/425F/Gas

7 for 10 mins, turning once.

Meanwhile put the flour, salt and a little egg in a small bowl and beat well. Gradually add the remaining egg and milk, a little at a time, and beat well after each addition, to make a smooth batter. Add herbs

Remove the tin from the oven and shake to loosen sausages. Pour batter over and return to the oven. Cook for further 30-40 mins, until well-risen and golden brown.

Serve immediately.

Approx cost £ 2.20

VEGETABLE COBBLER

1 tbsp oil
1 onion, sliced
3 leeks, washed and sliced
4 carrots, peeled and sliced
1oz/25g butter or margarine
1oz/25g plain flour
1 tbsp mustard
salt and pepper
1/2 pint/300ml milk
4 tbsp orange juice
1/4 pint/150ml natural yogurt

FOR THE COBBLER TOPPING

8oz/225g self-raising flour
2oz/50g margarine
1/4 pint/150ml milk
salt and pepper

METHOD

Heat oil in a pan and fry onions until softened.
Add leeks and carrots a for further 5 mins and
fry for further 10 mins until vegetables are tender, but not browned. Add butter and when it
has melted add flour and stir well to coat veggies. Cook for 1 min before adding mustard,
seasonings, milk and juice. Bring slowly to the
boil, stirring until thickened. Cover and simmer
for 10 mins, until vegetables are cooked, stirring occasionally.

Meanwhile make topping. Put flour in a bowl
and add margarine. Rub in with fingertips. Add
enough milk to make a firm scone dough. Turn
onto a lightly floured surface and knead gently.
Roll out to $1/2$ inch/1 cm thickness and use a
2in/5cm round cutter to stamp out circles.
Stir yogurt into the vegetable mixture and
transfer to an ovenproof dish. Arrange the
scone rounds, slightly overlapping, round the
edge of the dish. Brush with a little milk and
cook at 220C/425F/Gas 7 for 25 mins, until
topping is golden brown.

Approx cost £2.40

SPAGHETTI AND SAUSAGE BAKE

8oz/225g spaghetti
1lb/450g chipolata sausages,
2 tbsp oil
1 onion, sliced
1 clove garlic, crushed
2 tbsp plain flour
1 397g can chopped tomatoes with herbs
salt and pepper
2oz/50g cheese, grated

METHOD

Cook spaghetti in lightly salted boiling water
according to pack instructions. Drain. Grill or
fry sausages, drain on kitchen paper and cut
into thick slices.
Heat oil and fry onion and garlic until softened.
Add the plain flour and cook for 1 min. Add
chopped tomatoes and seasonings and bring
to the boil. Simmer for 10-15 mins, until thickened. Stir in the cooked spaghetti and
sausages and mix well.
Turn into an ovenproof dish
and sprinkle with cheese.
Cook at 200C/400F/Gas
6 for 15-20 mins, until
golden brown. Serve with
garlic bread.
Approx cost £2.50

PORK CHOPS WITH APPLE

1 dessert apple, finely sliced
1 onion, finely sliced
¼ pint/150ml dry cider
2 tbsp oil
1 tsp dried mixed herbs
¼ tsp ground cinnamon
salt and pepper
4 spare rib chops

METHOD

Mix the sliced apple, onion, cider, oil, herbs, spices and seasonings together in a shallow dish. Add chops, make sure they are covered in the marinade, and chill for at least two hours. Grill the chops for 8-10 mins on one side, regularly basting with the marinade. Turn chops over, baste again and grill second side until cooked through. Serve hot with mash and peas.
Approx cost £2.80

HOMEBURGERS

12oz/350g minced beef
3oz/75g fresh breadcrumbs
1 onion, finely chopped
2 tbsp tomato puree
salt and pepper
2 tsp dried mixed
herbs
1 egg, beaten

METHOD

Put mince, breadcrumbs, onion, puree seasonings, herbs and egg in a bowl and beat together (or whizz in a processor). Use cold, damp hands to shape into four burgers. Cook under a hot grill for 5 mins each side, depending on how rare you like them, until cooked.

Serve in a toasted bun and top with slices of cheese, a fried egg, rashers of bacon or beans.

Approx cost £1.40

CHUNKY CHICKEN PARCELS

1 8oz/225g pack puff pastry
1 tbsp oil
1 onion, roughly chopped
4 rashers rindless streaky bacon, chopped
1 large chicken breast, cut into chunks
1 tsp dried mixed herbs
4 tbsp Elmlea double cream
salt and pepper
1 beaten egg or milk to glaze

METHOD

Roll out the pastry to a 12in/30cm square
and cut into 4 smaller 6in/15cm squares.
Heat oil and fry onion and bacon until starting
to brown. Add chicken and fry for further 5-10
mins until chicken is cooked through. Add
herbs, cream and seasonings and mix well.
Leave to cool slightly. Share between the four
pastry squares, putting the mixture in the centre.

Brush the edges with egg and bring all four
corners over the filling to meet on top. Pinch
the seams together but leave a small opening
to allow the steam to escape. Brush with egg
or milk and lift carefully onto a baking sheet.
Cook at 200C/400F/Gas 6 for 25-30 mins,
until well-risen and golden. Serve hot or cold.

Approx cost £2.50

TIP: Long life alternatives to cream are often
on special offer and whether it's single or double, it'll come in handy for pasta and meat
sauces and for pouring over puds.

VEGETABLE LASAGNE

1 tbsp oil
1 onion, chopped
2 cloves garlic, crushed
8oz/225g mushrooms, sliced
4 courgettes, sliced
1 red pepper, de-seeded and chopped
1 tsp dried mixed Italian herbs
2 397g can chopped tomatoes
2 tbsp tomato puree
salt and pepper
2oz/50g butter
2oz/50g plain flour
1 pint/600ml milk
6oz/175g cheese, grated
8 sheets no-cook lasagne

METHOD

Heat oil and fry onions and garlic until softened. Add mushrooms, courgettes and pepper
and fry for further 10 mins, until vegetables
are tender. Add herbs, chopped tomatoes,
puree and seasonings, bring to the boil and
simmer for 10-15 mins, until mixture has
thickened and vegetables are cooked.
Melt the butter in a saucepan and stir in flour.
Cook for 1 min.
Remove from
heat and add the
milk, a little at a

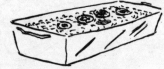

time, beating well after each addition. Return to the heat and bring to the boil, stirring all the time, until thickened. Remove from heat and stir in 4oz/100g of the grated cheese.

Spoon half the vegetable mixture into an oven-proof dish and level the top. Cover with four sheets of lasagne. Pour half the sauce over the top, spreading right to the edges.

Spread the rest of the vegetable mix over and top with last four sheets of lasagne. Spoon remaining sauce on top and scatter cheese over. Cook at 180C/350F/Gas 4 for 40-45 mins until golden brown. Serve hot with a green salad.

Approx cost £3.80

MEATBALLS IN BARBECUE SAUCE

1 lb/450g beef mince
1 clove garlic, crushed
8 spring onions, finely chopped
1 egg, beaten
salt and pepper
oil for frying
2 tbsp tomato puree
1 tbsp sugar
2 tbsp red wine, or vinegar
1/2 tsp chilli powder
1/4 pint/150ml beef stock
1 tsp cornflour

METHOD

Mix the beef, garlic, 2 spring onions, egg and seasoning together and use damp hands to roll into walnut-sized balls.

Heat oil and shallow-fry the meatballs, a few at a time, until browned on all sides. Lift out and drain on kitchen paper

Pour away excess oil but leave about 1 tbsp in the pan. Fry remaining spring onions until softened. Add puree, sugar, wine or vinegar, chilli powder and stock, plus 1 tbsp water. Bring to the boil and simmer for 3 mins.

Mix the cornflour with a little water and add to the sauce, stirring all the time. Return the meatballs to the pan and cook for further 5 mins, until cooked. Serve hot with rice or noodles.

Approx cost £2.20

SPICY CHICKEN WINGS

2 tbsp tomato puree
1/2 tsp ground coriander
1/2 tsp ground cumin
2 tbsp soy sauce
1 tbsp brown sugar
salt and pepper
12 chicken wings

METHOD

Mix tomato puree, coriander, cumin, soy and sugar, seasonings together in a bowl. Add the chicken wings and coat well. Leave to marinate for at least one hour

Arrange chicken in a small roasting tin and cook at 200C/400F/Gas 6 for 30m-40 mins, brushing occasionally with the marinade.

Serve hot or cold with a salad or fried rice

Approx cost £ 2.50

SPICY BEAN PIE

1 tbsp oil
1 onion, chopped
2 cloves garlic, crushed
4 carrots, peeled and diced
1 tbsp soy sauce
2 tbsp tomato puree
1 tsp dried mixed herbs
1 440g can mixed spicy beans
2oz/50g brown or white rice, cooked
1/2 pint/300ml vegetable stock
1lb/450g potatoes, peeled and diced
1oz/25g butter

METHOD

Heat oil and fry onions and garlic until soft-ened. Add diced carrots and fry for 5 mins until just tender. Add soy, puree, herbs, beans and rice and stir well. Add stock and bring to the boil. Reduce heat and simmer for 20-30 mins, until mixture has thickened.

Meanwhile cook potatoes in lightly salted boiling water until tender. Mash with the butter until smooth and creamy, adding a little milk as well.

Transfer the bean mixture to an ovenproof dish and level the top, Spread potato over and cook 180C/350F/Gas 4 for 30-40 mins, until crisp.

Approx cost £1.80

TIP: If mash is on the menu, cut the peeled potatoes into small cubes as they cook quicker and save on fuel.

SWEET AND SOUR PORK

1oz/25g plain flour
1 tsp ground ginger
salt and pepper
4 pork chops, cut into cubes
1 tbsp oil
1 onion, chopped
2 carrots, peeled and thinly sliced
1 green pepper, de-seeded and sliced
1/2 pint/300ml chicken stock
1 227g can pineapple pieces
2 tbsp soy sauce
2 tbsp vinegar
salt and pepper

METHOD

Mix the flour, ginger and seasonings together in a bowl and toss the pork cubes until evenly coated.

Heat oil and fry onion until softened. Add carrots and pepper and fry for 5 mins until just tender. Transfer to a casserole dish. Fry the pork in the same pan until browned all over. Add stock, pineapple and juice and bring to the boil, stirring. Simmer for 2 mins and add to casserole. Add soy, vinegar and seasonings and cook in the oven at 160C/325F/Gas 3 for 1-1^1/$_2$ hours. Serve with rice.

Approx cost £3.00

CHEAT'S CANNELONI.

12 sheets lasagne
4oz/100g mushrooms, chopped
1 7oz can tuna chunks, drained
1 tbsp tomato puree
1 tbsp oil
1 onion, finely chopped
2 cloves garlic, crushed
1 tsp dried mixed Italian herbs
1 397g can chopped tomatoes with onions and peppers
salt and pepper
3 oz/75g cheese, grated

METHOD

Cook the lasagne sheets in lightly salted boiling water, drain and cold rinse. Cover. Put mushrooms in a pan with a little water and simmer until tender. Pour off as much liquid as possible before adding drained, flaked tuna and the tomato puree. Stir together to make thick filling.

Put a spoonful of the mixture along the centre of each lasagne sheet and roll up to make a sausage shape. Arrange in a shallow dish, in a single layer if possible.

Heat oil and fry onion and garlic until softened. Add herbs, canned tomatoes and seasonings and simmer for 5-10 mins, until slightly thickened. Pour over the 'canneloni' scatter cheese over and cook at 190C/375F/Gas 5 for 20-25 mins, until golden brown. Serve with a salad and garlic bread.

Approx cost £2.70

GOULASH AND DUMPLINGS

1 tbsp oil
2 onions, sliced
2 cloves garlic, crushed
1lb/450g stewing steak, cubed
1 green pepper, de-seeded and sliced
1 397g can chopped tomatoes with herbs
3/4pint/450ml beef stock
2 tbsp tomato puree

2 tsp paprika
salt and pepper
6oz/175g plain flour
3oz/75g beef suet
2 tsp dried mixed herbs
salt and pepper

METHOD

Heat oil and fry onions
and garlic until softened
and starting to brown in
an ovenproof dish. Add
cubed meat and fry until
browned all over. Add pepper
and fry for further 3 mins, until
just tender. Pour canned tomatoes and stock over. Add puree,
paprika and seasonings and
bring gently to the boil. Transfer to the oven
and cook at 170C/325F/Gas 3 for $1^{1}/_{2}$
hours.

Mix the flour, suet, herbs and seasonings
together in a bowl. Add enough cold water to
make a firm dough. Use hands to roll into 8
balls.

Remove goulash from oven and arrange
dumplings on the top. Return to the oven for
further 30 mins until risen and cooked. Serve
hot with noodles.

Approx cost £ 3.20

STICKY CHICKEN DRUMSTICKS

2 tbsp oil
1 onion, chopped
1 clove garlic, crushed
2 tbsp tomato puree
2 tbsp vinegar
3 tbsp honey
1 tsp dried mixed herbs
1/2 tsp chilli powder
1/4 pint/150ml chicken stock
8 chicken drumsticks

METHOD

Heat oil and fry onion and garlic until softened.
Add puree, vinegar, honey, herbs, chilli powder
and stock, bring to the boil and simmer for 15-
20 mins, until starting to thicken.
Arrange the drumsticks in a roasting tin and
pour sauce over. Use a pastry brush to brush
sauce over the chicken and cook at
190C/375f Gas 5 for 1 1/4 hours. Brush occasionally with more sauce to keep chicken moist
and sticky. Serve hot or cold, or finish on a
barbecue.

Approx cost £2.20

BACON AND LEEK ROLY POLY

12oz/350g self-raising flour
6oz/75g beef suet
2 tsp dried mixed herbs
salt and pepper
2 large leeks, finely chopped
8oz/225g rindless streaky bacon, chopped

METHOD

Put flour, suet, herbs and
seasonings in a bowl and
add enough water to make
a firm dough. Turn onto a
lightly floured surface and
knead gently. Roll out to a rectangular shape
about 1/2in/1cm thick.
Scatter chopped leeks all over in an even layer
and repeat with the chopped bacon. Carefully
roll up from one side like a Swiss roll. Wrap
loosely in greaseproof paper, leaving room to
swell and wrap in a layer of foil. Put 1 in/2cm
water in a roasting tin. Stand roly poly in and
cover tin with foil. Cook at 190C/375F/Gas 5
for 1 hour, until risen and cooked. Lift out of
tin, unwrap carefully before slicing and serving
hot with green vegetables
Approx cost £1.90

TIP: The suet takes the place of spuds, so
just serve with veggies.

LIVER AND BACON STROGANOFF

2 tbsp plain flour
1 tsp dried mixed herbs
salt and pepper
1lb/450g lamb's liver, cut into strips
1 tbsp oil
8oz/225g rindless streaky bacon, chopped
2 onions, sliced
1 397g can chopped tomatoes with herbs
¼ pint/150ml soured cream

METHOD

Mix flour, herbs and seasonings together in a bowl and toss liver until evenly coated.

Heat oil and fry bacon and onions until starting to brown. Add liver and fry gently for further 5 mins.

Pour tomatoes over and simmer for 5-10 mins until meat is cooked. Reduce heat and stir in the soured cream. Heat through but do not allow to boil and serve hot.

Approx cost £ 2.75

CHEESEY AUBERGINE BAKE

2 aubergines
2 tbsp plain flour
2 tbsp oil
2 onions, cut into rings
2 cloves garlic, crushed

1 397g can chopped tomatoes
2 eggs, beaten
4oz/100g cheese, grated
2 tbsp natural yogurt
1 tsp dried mixed Italian herbs
salt and pepper
2 tbsp Parmesan cheese, grated

METHOD

Wash and slice the aubergines. Toss slices in
the flour until evenly coated. Heat oil and fry, a
few slices at a time until softened and starting
to brown. Drain on kitchen paper. Add more oil
if necessary.

Add onion rings to the pan and fry with garlic
until softened. Add tomatoes and cook for further 10 mins, until thickened. Remove from
heat and allow to cool.

Beat the eggs, cheese and yogurt together.
Add herbs and seasonings and the tomato mixture and stir well.

Put a layer of aubergines in the bottom of an
ovenproof dish and pour some of the sauce
over and sprinkle with a little Parmesan.

Continue to layer up aubergines and sauce, finishing with a layer of sauce and cheese. Cook
at 180C/350F/Gas 4 for 30-35 mins, until
golden brown and bubbling. Serve hot.

Approx cost £3.00

CHICKEN CRISP

4oz/100g dried pasta shapes
6oz/75g broccoli, cut into small florets
1 leek, cut into slices
2oz/50g butter
2 tbsp oil
1 large chicken breast, cut into cubes
1oz/25g flour
3/4 pint/450ml milk
salt and pepper
2 packs plain crisps
2oz/50g cheese, grated

METHOD

Cook the pasta in lightly salted
boiling water for 5 mins. Add broc-
coli and leeks and cook for further 5 mins, until
pasta and vegetables are tender. Drain well
and keep warm.

Put butter and oil in the warm pan and heat
gently. Fry chicken for 8-10 mins, until cooked
through. Add flour and stir well. Cook for 1 min
and lift off heat. Gradually add the milk a little
at a time, beating well after each addition.
Return to the heat and bring to the boil, stirring all the time until thickened Stir in pasta
and vegetables and heat through.

Transfer to an ovenproof dish and level top.
Scatter crisps over the top in an even layer
before sprinkling with grated cheese and pop-

ping under a hot grill until cheese melts and browns. Serve immediately.

Approx cost £3.20

NUTTY FRITTERS

2 onions, grated
1 tbsp dried mixed herbs
1 tsp ground coriander
1 tsp ground cumin
salt and pepper
12oz/350g mixed nuts, finely chopped
2 eggs, beaten
3oz/75g fresh breadcrumbs
oil for frying

METHOD

Mix onions, herbs, spices and seasonings together in a bowl. Add nuts, eggs and breadcrumbs and stir until evenly mixed. Divide into four equal pieces. Use hands to shape into four, flattish round fritters. Heat oil and shallow fry fritters until cooked through and browned all over. Serve hot with canned chopped tomatoes, or a mixed salad.

Approx cost £1.75

TIP: A cracking way to use up nuts left over after Christmas. Shell and roughly chop, pop into a polybag and hit with rolling pin, or put into a processor and whizz.

SAUSAGE HOT POT

1lb/450g thick pork sausages
1 onion, sliced
4oz /100g rindless streaky bacon, roughly
chopped
2 cloves garlic, crushed
4 sticks celery, chopped
1 397g can chopped tomatoes
2 tbsp tomato puree
1 425g can chilli beans
1 450g can baked beans
2 tsp dried mixed herbs
salt and pepper

METHOD

Grill sausages until cooked and browned. Allow
to cool before cutting into thick slices.
Put onion, bacon and garlic in a
pan and fry until starting to
brown, adding a little oil if
necessary. Add celery and
cook for further 3 mins.
Pour tomatoes over. Add
puree, herbs, beans, and seasoning and bring gently to the
boil. Add sliced sausages and
simmer for 15 mins, until
hot through. Serve immediately with mash or rice.
Approx cost £3.00

TOMATO SLICE

8oz/225g puff pastry
6oz/175g cheese, thinly sliced
1 onion, cut into rings
4 tomatoes, sliced

METHOD

Roll pastry into an 10in/25cm square and
transfer to a lightly greased baking sheet.
Arrange cheese slices over pastry. Scatter
onion rings and tomato slices over and cook at
200C/400F/Gas 6 for 15-20 mins until well
risen and golden brown. Serve hot with green
salad or beans.

Approx cost £ 1.50

SPAGHETTI CARBONARA

12oz/350g spaghetti
4 eggs, beaten
1/4pint/150ml single cream
8oz/225g rindless streaky bacon, roughly
chopped
6oz/175g cheese, grated
salt and pepper

METHOD

Cook pasta in lightly salted boiling water until
just tender.
Beat eggs and cream together in a bowl. Fry
or grill the bacon until crisp.

Drain the pasta and return to the pan. Pour egg mixture over, add bacon, 4oz/100g cheese and seasonings and toss well, until evenly coated. (The heat of the pan and spaghetti will cook the egg.)

Serve immediately, topped with the remaining cheese.

Approx cost £ 2.50

CHICKEN RISOTTO

1 tbsp oil
1 onion, finely chopped
2 cloves garlic, crushed
2 chicken breasts, thinly sliced
3 tbsp white wine (optional)
10oz/275g rice
1 pint/600ml chicken stock
4oz/100g mushrooms, thinly sliced
1 red pepper, de-seeded and sliced
4 rashers bacon, finely chopped
salt and pepper

METHOD

Heat oil and fry onions and garlic until softened. Add chicken strips and fry until meat has turned white. Add wine and simmer for 5-10 mins.

Add rice and most of the stock, cover and simmer for further 15-20 mins, until rice is cooked. Add more stock if necessary.
Meanwhile fry mushrooms, pepper and bacon in a pan until cooked and browned. Stir into the cooked rice mixture, season and serve.
Approx cost £3.50

QUICK CHILLI

1 tbsp oil
1 onion, chopped
2 cloves garlic, crushed
1lb/450g minced beef
2 397g cans chopped tomatoes with onions and peppers
2 tbsp tomato puree
1 tsp chilli powder, according to taste
salt and pepper
1 450g can baked beans

METHOD

Heat oil and fry onion and garlic until softened. Add mince and fry until browned all over. Add chopped tomatoes, puree chilli and seasonings, reduce heat and simmer for 20-30 mins, until mixture has thickened.
Add baked beans, stir well and cook for further 5-10 mins until they are hot. Serve with rice.
Approx cost £ 2.30

SAUSAGE PUFFS

8oz/225g puff pastry
4 tbsp tomato ketchup, or mustard
8 pork or beef sausages
egg or milk to glaze

METHOD

Roll pastry out to a 10in/25cm square and
cut onto four smaller equal squares.Cut each
one in half diagonaly to make 8 triangles.
Brush each one with tomato ketchup or mustard. Brush edges with milk or egg. Put a
sausage across the centre and fold corners of
pastry over. Press well to seal edges. Brush
with egg or milk, stand on a lightly greased
baking sheet and cook at 200C/400F/Gas 6
for 20-25 mins, until pastry has risen and
sausages are cooked.
Approx cost £ 2.10

SMOKED MACKEREL PASTA

12oz/350g Penne pasta
2 smoked peppered mackerel fillets
4oz/100g cream cheese
¼ pint/150ml natural
yogurt
2 tbsp lemon juice
2 tomatoes, finely
chopped

METHOD

Cook pasta in lightly salted boiling water until just tender, following pack instructions.
Flake the mackerel fillets and remove any bones. Beat the cream cheese, yogurt and lemon juice together.
Drain the pasta and return to the pan. Add mackerel and cheese mixture and cook for 5 mins, until hot. Serve immediately, topped with the chopped fresh tomatoes.
Approx cost £ 2.60

POTATO PIE

1lb/450g puff pastry
2lb/900g potatoes, peeled and thinly sliced
1 onion, peeled and cut into rings
2 tbsp dried mixed herbs
salt and pepper
¼ pint/150ml double cream
2 cloves garlic, crushed
1 egg, beaten
3oz/75g cheese, grated
egg or milk to
glaze

METHOD

Roll out 3/4 of the pastry and use to line the base and sides of an 8in/20cm deep sided, spring release flan tin. Roll out remaining pastry until large enough to make the lid. Chill.

Add the sliced potatoes to lightly salted boiling water, cook for 2 mins, before draining and cold-rinsing. Allow to drain and cool.

Arrange a layer of sliced potatoes over the base of the pastry case. Scatter some of the onion rings over and a sprinkling of herbs and seasonings over the top. Gradually build up layers of potatoes, onions, herbs and seasonings until the pastry case is full.

Whisk cream with garlic and egg and pour over layered vegetables. Top with grated cheese. Cover with pastry lid and seal edges well. Brush with egg or milk. Make leaves from pastry trimmings and decorate top. Glaze again and cook at 200C/400F/Gas 6 for 40-45 mins, until browned. Serve hot or cold with salad or green vegetables

Approx cost £ 2.40

HONEY GLAZED LAMB

4 lamb chump chops
salt and pepper
2 oz/50g butter or margarine
2 tbsp honey
1 tsp coarse grain mustard

METHOD

Arrange chops on a foil-lined grill pan. Season well. Beat butter, honey and mustard together until soft. Spread half of the mixture over the

chops and grill for 5 mins. Turn over, glaze
again and grill second side, brushing with the
glaze occasionally. Serve with jacket potatoes
and green veg.

Approx cost £ 2.40

PAN COOKED KIDNEYS

1oz/25g butter
12oz/350g lamb's kidneys, peeled and thinly
sliced
1 onion, thinly sliced
4oz/100g rindless streaky bacon, roughly
chopped
1/2oz/15g plain flour
1/2 pint/300ml beef or lamb stock
1 tbsp tomato puree
salt and pepper
1 tbsp dried mixed herbs

METHOD

Melt butter in a frying pan, add sliced kidneys
and fry for 3-5 mins, until cooked. Remove
from pan. Add onion and bacon and fry until
starting to brown. Add flour and stir well. Cook
for 2 mins before gradually stirring in stock.
Add puree, seasonings and herbs and bring
gently to the boil. Return the kidneys to the
pan and simmer for 15 mins. Serve hot with
noodles or macaroni.

Approx cost £ 1.95

PORK WITH APPLES

4oz/100g mushrooms, sliced
2 cooking apples, peeled and sliced
1 onion, thinly sliced
4 pork chops
4 tbsp cider or apple juice
salt and pepper
2oz/50g fresh breadcrumbs
2oz/50g cheese, grated

METHOD

Scatter the mushrooms, apples and
onion over the base of an ovenproof dish. Arrange the chops on
top. Pour cider or apple juice over
and add enough water to half
cover the chops. Season well. Mix
the breadcrumbs and cheese together and
scatter over the top. Cook at
190C/375F/Gas 5 for 40-45 mins, until
meat is cooked and top browned. Serve hot
with vegetables.
Approx cost £ 2.75

TUNA FISHCAKES

1 200g/7oz can tuna in brine
12oz/350g mashed potato
1 egg. beaten
2 tsp mixed dried herbs
1/2 tsp ground nutmeg

salt and pepper
2 tbsp milk
4 tbsp plain flour
oil for shallow frying

METHOD

Drain and flake the tuna into a bowl. Add
mash, egg, herbs, nutmeg and seasonings and
mix well. Add a little milk if the mixture is too
dry.

Use damp hands to shape the mixture into 8
fishcakes. Dip into the flour and then into hot
oil. Fry on both sides until crisp and golden
brown. Drain on kitchen paper and serve
immediately.

Approx cost £ 1.20

SPANISH TORTILLA

1lb/450g potatoes
1 tbsp oil
1 onion, cut into rings
1 clove garlic, crushed
1 red pepper, de-seeded and sliced
6 eggs. beaten
2 tsp dried mixed herbs
salt and
pepper

METHOD

Peel, cube and cook potatoes until just tender in lightly salted boiling water. Drain. Heat oil and fry onion and garlic until softened. Add potatoes and pepper fry for 1 min.

Mix eggs together with 1 tbsp water, herbs and seasonings and pour over potato and pepper mixture. Reduce heat and cook gently for 15 mins, until set.

Pop under a hot grill to brown and set the top and serve hot or cold with green salad or vegetables.

Approx cost £1.60

PAN HAGGARTY

3 tbsp oil
1 onion, thinly sliced
1 clove garlic, crushed
1lb/450g minced beef
4oz/100g mushrooms. sliced
2 tbsp tomato puree
2lb/1kg potatoes, peeled and thinly sliced
4oz/100g cheese, grated
1/2 pint/300ml beef stock

METHOD

Heat 1 tbsp oil and fry onion and garlic until softened. Add mince and cook until browned all over. Add mushrooms and

tomato puree and cook for further 3 mins. Lift
out of pan and reserve.

Clean pan. Brush with remaining oil and
arrange half the potatoes over the base.
Scatter half the cheese over. Spoon the mince
mixture over and top with grated cheese.
Arrange potatoes, slight;y overlapping, on top.
Pour stock over and cover. Cook on a low heat
for 45-50 mins before removing lid and cooking for 5 mins. Brush potatoes with a little oil
and pop under a hot grill to brown the top.
Serve hot with green vegetables.

Approx cost £ 2.80

BEEF GOULASH

1oz/25g plain flour
1 tsp mustard powder
1 tsp paprika
salt and pepper
1lb/450g stewing or braising steak, cut into
cubes
2 tbsp oil
2 onions, sliced
2 cloves garlic, crushed
1 red pepper, de-seeded and sliced
1 green pepper, de-seeded and sliced
1 397g can chopped tomatoes
2 tbsp tomato puree
1 pint/600ml beef stock
¼ pint/150ml soured cream

METHOD

Mix flour, mustard, paprika and seasonings together in a bowl. Add the cubes of meat and toss until evenly coated

Heat oil and fry steak until browned on all sides. Transfer to an ovenproof casserole dish. Fry onions and garlic in the same pan until softened. Add peppers and fry for further 5 mins. Add to the meat and with canned tomatoes, puree and stock. Cover and cook at 170C/325F/Gas 3 for 2 hours, until meat is tender.

Pour the soured cream over just before serving.

Approx cost £3.40

VEGETABLE CURRY

2 tbsp oil
1 bunch spring onions, chopped
2 cloves garlic, crushed
4oz/100g potatoes, diced
2 carrots, peeled and diced
4oz/100g cauliflower, cut into florets
4oz/100g green beans, topped and tailed and cut into 1in/2cm lengths
1 tsp chilli powder
1 tbsp Thai curry powder
according to taste
salt and pepper
1 397g can chopped tomatoes

METHOD

Heat oil and fry onions and garlic until starting to brown. Add all other vegetables and stir fry for 2 mins. Add chilli and curry powder and seasonings. Pour tomatoes over, cover and cook gently for 15 mins. Remove lid and cook for further 5 mins. Check seasoning. Add some natural yogurt if it's too hot and serve with rice.

Approx cost £1.90

GNOCCHI

1 1/2 pints/ 900ml milk
6oz/175g semolina
salt and pepper
1 tsp ground nutmeg
6oz/175g cheese, grated
2 tbsp Parmesan cheese, grated
1 egg yolk
2 tbsp milk

METHOD

Heat the milk until just boiling. Sprinkle semolina over, stirring all the time. Add seasonings and nutmeg and simmer until mixture thickens and becomes solid. Remove from heat and beat in 4oz/100g of the grated cheese. Pour into a Swiss roll tin, spread out into an even layer and leave to cool. Use a 2in/5cm round cutter to stamp out circles. Arrange

them, slightly overlapping, in a lightly greased
ovenproof dish.
Beat the egg yolk and milk together and pour
over. Sprinkle with remaining grated cheese
and top with Parmesan. Cook at
200C/400F/Gas 6 for 30-40 mins, until gold-
en brown. Serve immediately with a mixed
salad.
Approx cost £ 2.00

FISH VOL-AU-VENTS

8oz/225g puff pastry
egg or milk for glazing
1 oz/25g butter or margarine
1 onion, chopped
4oz/100g mushrooms, finely sliced
4oz/100g cod or haddock, skinned, boned
and cut into cubes
4oz/100g smoked cod or haddock, skinned,
boned and cut into
cubes
1oz/25g plain flour
1/2 pint/300ml milk
2 tbsp Pernod (optional)
salt and pepper

METHOD

Roll pastry into a 10in/25cm square and cut
into four smaller equal squares. Mark a smaller square 1/2 in/1 cm inside the edges of

each one. 'Knock up' the sides with a knife and arrange on a baking sheet. Brush with egg or milk and cook at 200C/400F/Gas 6 for 15-20 mins until puffed up and golden brown. As they come out of the oven lift out the 'lid' that was marked earlier to allow the steam to escape.

Melt butter in a saucepan and cook onions until softened. Add mushrooms and fry for 2 mins. Add fish and fry gently until fish is cooked and flakes easily.

Add flour and stir well. Gradually add the milk, a little at a time, and mixing well after each addition. Add Pernod and seasonings and bring gently to the boil, stirring all the time. Allow to simmer for 2 mins.

Put spoonfuls of the fish mixture inside the pastry cases and top with the 'lid'. Serve hot with green vegetables.

Approx cost £ 3.20

CHICKEN THIGHS IN YOGURT

8 chicken thighs
2 tsp paprika
salt and pepper
¼ pint/150ml natural yogurt

METHOD

Put the chicken thighs in a large bowl. Stir the paprika and seasonings into the yogurt and pour over the chicken. Turn to coat evenly and chill for 3 hours.

Arrange the chicken in a roasting tin, still coated in the yogurt and cook at 190C/375F/Gas 5 for 40-45 mins, until cooked and browned.

Serve hot or cold with rice and salad

Approx cost £ 1.60

LAMB JALOUSIE

8oz/225g puff pastry
12oz/350g minced lamb
1 oz/25g fresh breadcrumbs
1 onion, finely chopped
1 tsp dried rosemary
1 tbsp tomato puree
2 eggs beaten
salt and pepper

METHOD

Roll pastry into two 9x5in/22x12cm rectangles.

Mix the lamb, breadcrumbs, onion, herbs, puree, half the egg and seasonings together in a bowl. Arrange the mixture down the centre of one of the pastry rectangles and brush the edges with the beaten egg.

Lift the other piece of pastry on top and press the edges well together. 'Knock up' the edges with a knife and make slits, every inch or so across the top. Brush with more egg and cook

at 200C/400F/Gas 6 for 30-40 mins, until
meat has cooked and pastry is golden brown
and well risen. Serve hot or cold.
Approx cost £2.50

TUNA SOUFFLE

1 1/2oz/40g butter
1 1/2oz/40g plain flour
3/4 pint/450ml milk
4 eggs separated
2oz/50g cheese, grated
1 200g can tuna in brine, drained and flaked
salt and pepper
1 tsp dried mixed herbs
1/2 tsp paprika
1 tsp ground nutmeg

METHOD

Lightly grease a 1 1/2 pint/900ml souffle dish.
Melt butter in a saucepan, add flour and cook
for 1 min. Remove from heat and gradually add
milk, a little at a time, beating well after each
addition. Return to heat and bring to the boil
stirring all the time until thickened. Allow to cool
slightly before beating in egg yolks. Stir in
cheese, tuna, seasonings, herbs, paprika and
nutmeg.
Whisk egg whites until stiff. Beat 2 tbsp into the
cheese sauce to loosen mixture before folding in
the rest of the egg whites with a metal spoon.

Cook at 200C/400F/Gas 6 for 30 mins, until set, risen and browned. Serve immediately.
Approx cost £2.10

PASTA PESTO

12oz/350g pasta spirals
1 tbsp oil
1 onion, finely chopped
2 cloves garlic, crushed
4 tbsp Pesto sauce
2 tbsp single cream
2 tbsp Parmesan cheese
salt and pepper

METHOD

Cook the pasta in lightly salted, boiling water until just tender.
Heat oil and fry onion and garlic until softened.
Stir in Pesto, cream, cheese and seasonings and heat gently. Do not allow to boil.
Drain the pasta, return to the pan and pour sauce over. Toss well and serve immediately.
Approx cost £1.70

SPEEDY PIZZA

1 28g pack bread or pizza dough mix
1 tbsp oil
2 onions finely chopped
2 cloves garlic, crushed
4 oz mushrooms, thinly sliced

1 397g can chopped tomatoes
3 tbsp tomato puree
2 tsp dried mixed Italian herbs
salt and pepper
2oz/50g peppered
salami
1 red pepper,
de-seeded and
sliced
4oz/100g
Mozzarella
cheese

METHOD

Follow pack instruc-
tions to make up dough and divide into four
smaller pieces or roll out to one large pizza
that can be sliced. Put on a lightly greased baking sheet.

Heat oil and fry onions and garlic until softened. Add mushrooms and fry for 2 mins, until
tender. Add chopped tomatoes, puree, herbs
and seasonings and simmer for 25-30 mins,
until thickened. Spread sauce over pizza bases.
Top with sliced salami, red pepper and
Mozzarella cheese.

Cook at 200C/40F/Gas 6 for 20-25 mins,
until cooked and golden brown. Serve hot or
cold with salad.

Approx cost £ 2.25

MUSHROOM AND NUT GOUGERE

2oz/50g margarine
¼ pint/150ml water
2 ½oz/65g plain or wholemeal flour
2 eggs
2oz/50g cheese, grated
2 tbsp oil
1 onion, chopped
2 cloves garlic, crushed
8oz/225g mushrooms, thinly sliced
1 tbsp flour
¼ pint/150ml vegetable stock
3oz/75g mixed walnuts and hazelnuts
2 tsp dried mixed herbs

METHOD

Melt the margarine in a saucepan, add water and bring to the boil. Add the flour all at once and beat quickly until mixture leaves the sides of the pan clean. Cool slightly and add the eggs, a little at a time, beating well after each addition, until shiny but still quite firm. (You may not need all the egg.)

Beat in the cheese and and spoon the mixture round the edge of a deep-sided ovenproof dish Heat the oil in a pan and fry the onion and garlic until softened. Add mushrooms and fry for further 3 mins. Stir in the flour and gradually add the stock, a little at a time. Bring to the boil, stirring all the time until thickened. Stir in most of the mixed nuts, reserving 3 tbsp for the top, and the herbs.

Put the mixture in the middle of the dish and sprinkle remaining nuts over. Cook at 200C/400F/Gas 6 for 40-45 mins, until well risen. Serve immediately

Approx cost £2.40

SPICY BEEF IN YOGURT

1lb/450g braising or stewing steak
1/2 pint/300ml natural yogurt
1 tbsp oil
1 onion, sliced
3 cloves garlic. roughly chopped
2 tsp ground coriander
1 tbsp Authentic curry powder
salt and pepper

METHOD

Put the meat between two sheets of grease-proof paper and pound with a rolling pin until thin. Cut into strips and put into a bowl with the yogurt. Cover and chill overnight.

Heat oil and fry onion and garlic until starting to brown. Add coriander and curry powder and cook for further 3 mins. Add beef and yogurt and stir well. Cover and simmer for 1 1/2 hours until meat is tender. Serve hot with rice.

Approx cost £2.75

TIP: Marinate tougher cuts of meat in yogurt or oil overnight to tenderise them.

MACARONI GRATIN

6oz/175g short cut macaroni
2oz/50g butter or margarine
2 large leeks, washed and thinly sliced
1oz/25g plain flour
1 pint/600ml milk
6oz/175g cheese, grated
salt and pepper
1oz/25g fresh breadcrumbs

METHOD

Cook macaroni in lightly salted boiling water until just tender and drain well.

Melt butter in a pan and fry leeks gently for a few mins until just tender. Stir in the flour and cook for 1 min. Remove pan from heat and gradually add milk, beating well after each addition. Return to the heat and bring to the boil stirring all the time. Simmer for 2 mins. Remove from heat and add 4oz/100g of the grated cheese and seasonings. Stir in the macaroni. Transfer mixture to an ovenproof dish. Mix the breadcrumbs with the remaining cheese and sprinkle over the top.

Cook at 190C/375F/Gas 5 for 30-40 mins, until bubbling and golden brown. Serve immediately.

Approx cost £2.25

CHAPTER FIVE
FEELING PECKISH?

FRITTATA

1 tbsp oil
4 eggs, beaten
4oz/100g frozen spinach, defrosted and
cooked
3 tomatoes, roughly chopped
1 large potato, cooked and diced
salt and pepper
1 tsp dried mixed herbs

METHOD

Heat oil in a frying pan. Pour in the beaten
eggs and stir for a few seconds. Allow to start
setting before scattering the spinach, tomatoes and potatoes evenly over the top.

Sprinkle seasonings and herbs over the top and cook gently for 4-5 mins, until the base is cooked. Then either turn the frittata over or pop under a hot grill to set the top.

Cut into quarters and serve hot or cold with a salad.

Approx cost £1.50

CLUB SANDWICHES

12 slices bread
4 tbsp mayonnaise
4 slices cooked chicken, or chicken roll
4 lettuce leaves
8 rashers rindless streaky bacon, grilled
4 tomatoes, thinly sliced

METHOD

Toast four slices of bread on both sides, but only toast the remaining eight slices on one side.

Spread the untoasted sides with the mayonnaise and lay four of them, toasted side down on the board. Top with chicken slices

Put the toasted slice on top. Then add a layer of crispy bacon, lettuce and tomato and top with the remaining slices, mayonnaise side down, to make four three-layered sandwiches. Press lightly and cut each sandwich into four triangles. Serve warm.

Approx cost £1.60

HAM AND POTATO LAYER

3oz/75g butter
4 tbsp fresh breadcrumbs
1 ¹/₂lb/675g potatoes
6oz/175g cooked ham, roughly chopped
6oz/175g cheese, grated
¼ pint/150ml milk

METHOD

Grease an 8inch/20cm spring form tin, or
ovenproof dish with a little of the butter and
sprinkle breadcrumbs over
Cook potatoes whole in lightly salted boiling
water. Drain, peel and cut into thick slices.
Cover the bottom of the tin with a layer of
potatoes, slightly overlapping each other. Melt
the remaining butter or marg and brush over
the spuds. Scatter some chopped ham and
grated cheese over. Season well. Continue lay-
ering up the potatoes, ham and cheese, finishing with a layer of potato topped with cheese.
Pour the milk over and brush with any remaining butter. Cook at 180C/350F/Gas 4 for
30-40 mins, until golden and bubbling. Turn
out of tin onto a plate, or serve
from the dish.

Approx cost £1.90

SOFT ROES ON TOAST

1lb/450g soft roes
8 slices bread
little butter for spreading
salt and pepper

METHOD

Put soft roes in a frying pan and cook gently
for 10 mins.
Toast the bread on both sides and spread with
butter. Put two slices on each plate
Put the frying pan under a hot grill to brown
and crisp the roes, turning once or twice,
before serving onto the toast. Eat immediately.
Approx cost £2.00

RED FLANNEL HASH

6 rashers rindless streaky bacon, chopped
1 onion, finely chopped
12oz/350g potatoes, cooked and mashed
6oz/175g cooked beetroot, diced
8oz/225g corned beef
2 tsp chopped fresh parsley, or 1 tbsp dried
herbs
2 tbsp milk
salt and pepper

METHOD

Fry the bacon and onion together in a frying
pan, adding a little oil if necessary. Lift out and

put into a mixing bowl. Add potatoes, beetroot, corned beef, parsley milk and seasonings. Mix well, return to the pan and press down firmly in an even layer. Cook for 15 mins, until the base is browned before serving.
Approx cost £1.80

BACON TOAD
3oz/75g plain flour
$1/2$ pint/300ml milk
2 eggs, beaten
salt and pepper
1 tsp dried mixed herbs
8oz/225g rindless streaky bacon, chopped

METHOD
Put flour into a bowl and beat in half the milk. Add eggs and rest of the milk, gradually, beating well after each addition. to make a smooth batter.
Season well and add herbs.
Fry bacon in a pan until crisp. Pour a little of the fat into an ovenproof dish, add bacon and put into a hot oven, 180C/350F/Gas 4 for 10 mins, until hot.
Pour batter over and return to oven for further 30-40 mins until well-risen and golden brown.
Serve with tinned tomatoes or beans
Approx cost £1.30

CROQUE MONSIEUR

8 slices thin-sliced bread,
2oz/50g butter or margarine
4 slices ham
4oz/100g grated cheese
oil for shallow frying

METHOD

Spread each slice of bread with butter or
marg. Top four slices with a slice of ham and
grated cheese. Put the four remaining slices
on top and press well together before cutting
off the crusts to seal the sandwich. Cut each
one into three equal fingers.

Heat the oil and shallow fry the sandwiches, a
few at a time, until crisp and golden brown.
Drain on kitchen paper and serve hot.

Approx cost 95p

PROVENCAL EGGS

1 tbsp oil
1 onion, chopped
1 clove garlic, crushed
1 red pepper, de-seeded and sliced
8oz/225g courgettes, sliced
1 397g can chopped tomatoes
with herbs
salt and pepper
4 eggs

METHOD

Heat oil in a frying pan and fry onion and garlic until softened. Add pepper and courgettes and cook for further 5 mins, until starting to soften. Add canned tomatoes and seasonings.and simmer for 3 mins. Make four dips in the mixture. Break an egg into each one and simmer gently until eggs set.
Approx cost £1.80

TIP: Serve at once or scatter 2oz/50g grated cheese over and pop under the grill to melt.

PATE PARCELS

8oz/225g puff pastry
8oz/225g liver pate
2 spring onions, finely chopped
1 egg, beaten

METHOD

Roll pastry out to a 12in/30cm square and cut onto sixteen 3in/8cm smaller squares Mix the liver pate with the spring onions and put a spoonful in the centre of each pastry square. Brush the edges with beaten egg and fold each one into a triangle. Seal the edges well and brush with

egg. Arrange on a lightly greased baking sheet and cook at 18OC/35OG/Gas 4 for 10-15 mins, until cooked and browned.
Serve hot.

Approx cost £1.50

QUICK EGGS BENEDICT

4 muffins, cut in half
4 slices lean ham, cut in half
8 eggs
4 tbsp mayonnaise
salt and pepper
paprika

METHOD

Lightly toast the muffins on both sides and arrange half a ham slice on each.
Poach the eggs, either in a poacher in which case you may have to cook two batches, or carefully break eggs into boiling water and simmer until set.
Turn out an egg on each muffin half and top with a spoonful of mayonnaise. Season and sprinkle a little paprika over. Serve immediately.

Approx cost £2.00

SAVOURY SCRAMBLED EGGS

4 tomatoes
1 tbsp oil
1 onion, finely chopped
4oz/100g luncheon meat, roughly chopped
3 eggs, beaten
salt and pepper
8 slices bread

METHOD

Put the tomatoes in a bowl and pour boiling
water over. Leave for 10 mins. When the skin
splits peel off and roughly chop the flesh.
Heat oil and fry onion until softened. Add tomatoes and meat and cook for 4-5 mins. Stir in
the eggs and seasonings and continue cooking
until eggs are set.
Toast the bread and serve hot with the eggs.
Approx cost £1.30

WELSH RAREBIT

8oz/225g cheese, grated
1oz/25g butter
1 tsp mustard powder
2 tbsp beer
salt and pepper
4 slices bread

METHOD

Put the cheese, butter, mustard powder, beer

and seasonings in a saucepan together and heat gently, stirring occasionally.

Toast the bread on both sides and spread the cheese mixture over the four slices. Put under a hot grill and cook until bubbling and golden brown.

Serve with tomatoes or beans.

Approx cost £ 1.30

CRISPY TUNA SANDWICHES

16 slices thin-sliced bread
2oz/50g butter or margarine
1 200g can tuna in brine
2oz/50g soft cheese spread
salt and pepper
2 eggs, beaten
1 tbsp milk
oil for shallow frying

METHOD

Cut 16 circles from the bread slices using a 3-4in/7.5-10.5 cutter, or scissors, and spread each with butter or marg.

Drain the tuna and remove any bones. Mash with a fork and beat in the cheese spread. Season well and spread over eight of the buttered bread circles. Top with the other circles to make eight sandwiches. Press edges together well.

Beat the eggs and milk together in a shallow

bowl. Heat the oil in a frying pan. Dip the sandwiches in the egg mixture and then into the hot oil. Shallow fry, turning once, until crisp on both sides. Drain on kitchen paper before serving hot with a tomato salad.

Approx cost £1.60

SAUSAGE STUFFED PITTAS

4 pitta breads, cut in half
8 thin sausages, cooked
2 tomatoes, sliced
4 lettuce leaves
3 tbsp mayonnaise or tomato ketchup

METHOD

Run the pitta breads quickly under the tap and pop them under the grill and cook both sides. Cut them in half, taking care as the steam can burn, and open out each half. Cut the sausages in half lengthways and pop 3 halves in each pitta pocket. Tuck in some tomato slices, torn lettuce and mayonnaise or ketchup. Serve warm.

Approx cost £1.40

QUICK SAUSAGE PIZZA

1lb/450g Lincolnshire or
Cumberland sausages,
4 thick slices bread
6 tbsp tomato

ketchup or relish
2oz/50g cheese, grated

METHOD

Grill sausages until browned and cooked through. Drain on kitchen paper.
Toast the bread on both sides and spread one side with the ketchup or relish. Slice the sausages lengthways and lay on top of bread. Scatter grated cheese over and pop back under the grill until the cheese is melted and bubbling. Serve hot.

Approx cost £1.70

SAVOURY STUFFED CROIS-SANTS

4 croissants
8 rashers rindless streaky bacon
4oz/100g cheese, grated
2 tomatoes, sliced

METHOD

Slice the croissants open and warm gently in the oven, or pop under the grill for a few seconds. Grill bacon until crisp and put two rashers inside each croissant. Sprinkle grated cheese over, add tomato slices and sandwich two halves together again. Serve warm.

Approx cost £1.50

MINI QUICHES

8oz/225g shortcrust pastry
8 rashers rindless streaky bacon, chopped
3 spring onions, chopped
6oz/175g cheese, grated
3 eggs, beaten
1/2 pint/300ml milk
salt and pepper

METHOD

Roll out the pastry on a floured surface and use a 3in/7.5cm round cutter to stamp out 24 circles. Line 2 12-hole bun tins with the pastry circles.

Fry the bacon and spring onions together in a frying pan until crisp and divide the mixture between the 24 pastry cases. Top each one with a little grated cheese.

Beat the eggs and seasonings together and spoon a little into each mini quiche.

Cook at 180C/350F/Gas 4 for 20-25 mins until set and browned. Serve hot or cold.

Approx cost £ 2.00

TIP: Pop any left-overs in the lunch box or freeze for another day.

SAUSAGE PIE

2 8oz/225g pieces puff pastry
8oz/225g sausage meat
1 onion, chopped
2oz/50g fresh breadcrumbs
1 egg, beaten
salt and pepper
3 eggs, hard boiled
1 tbsp milk, to glaze

METHOD

Roll out pastry to make two 12x6in/30x15cm rectangles. Place on a lightly greased baking sheet.

Mix sausage meat, onion, breadcrumbs, beaten egg and seasonings together. Spread half the mixture along the centre of one of the pastry rectangles

Cut the hard boiled eggs in half lengthways and lie along the top of the sausage meat, cut side down. Cover with the remaining sausage meat and press into a neat shape.

Moisten pastry edges with water and top with second rectangle. Seal edges well and brush with milk. Cook at 200C/400F/Gas 6 for 35-40 mins until cooked and browned. Serve hot or cold with warm beans or a salad.

Approx cost £ 1.50

SPEEDY SARDINE PATÉ

1 120g can sardines in oil
4oz/100g curd cheese
1 tbsp lemon juice
1 tbsp tomato puree or ketchup
pepper
4 slices bread

METHOD

Drain oil from sardines and discard. Split sardines open and remove backbone before putting in a bowl. Add curd cheese, lemon juice, tomato and pepper. Beat well together and chill.

Toast the bread on both sides. Slip a knife into the side of each slice and cut round the bread, halving the slice lengthways. Cut each half into 4 triangles and toast untoasted side. Serve warm with the paté.

Approx cost £1.50

SARNIES

Most people have a sandwich at lunchtime, whether it's something exotic from a sandwich bar near the office, or something more down to earth in a lunchbox. But they can get boring, so here's ten fab fillings to make a change but that won't cost the earth

BACON AND PEANUT BUTTER

Grill three rashers of bacon and drain on kitchen paper. Spread bread with peanut butter. Top one slice with bacon and second slice of bread.

CHOCOLATE SPREAD AND BANANA

Spread both slices of bread with chocolate spread. Mash one small banana with a little lemon juice, to prevent discolouration and spread over one slice. Sandwich two halves together.

CURRIED EGG MAYONNAISE

Hard boil an egg and rinse under cold water.
Shell and mash with 1 tbsp mayonnaise, a little
salt and 1/2 tsp curry paste, depending on
taste. Spread mixture over one slice of bread
or half a roll. Top with a lettuce leaf and other
slice.

CHEESE AND MARMALADE

Spread bread with butter and one slice with
thick cut marmalade. Top with sliced or grated
cheese and other slice of bread

PATE AND GHERKIN

Spread bread thinly with butter. Put pate or
liver pate spread in a bowl and beat in two finely chopped gherkins, according to taste. Spread
mixture over one slice, and slices of tomato
and top with remaining bread slice.

FISHY FINGERS

Grill two fish fingers and mash with a fork. Add
a little salt and pepper and 1 tsp either mayonnaise, tomato ketchup or tartare sauce. Top
with second slice of bread.

SAUSAGE AND
BEANS

Grill two pork
sausages and cut each

into three thin slices lengthways. Spread bread or rolls
thinly with butter and
arrange sliced
sausages on one slice.
Top with a spoonful of
cold baked beans and the second slice of
bread.

CHINESE CHICKEN

Butter two slices of bread with butter and
arrange sliced cold chicken, or chicken roll on
one half. Toss a handful of beansprouts and a
stalk of thinly sliced celery in a little soy sauce,
season well and scatter over the chicken. Top
with second slice.

SALMON AND CREAM CHEESE

Spread one slice of bread with spreading
salmon pate and top with a layer of thinly sliced
cucumber. Season. Spread the second slice
with cream cheese spread and place over the
cucumber.

CHEESE AND MARMITE

Spread two slices of bread with a thin layer of
butter. Spread one slice with marmite. Top
with grated cheese and sliced tomatoes before
putting second slice on top.

TIP: Don't be boring with your butties! Use granary or wholemeal bread, assorted rolls, croissants or French sticks. Kids love the mini Hovis rolls or pitta bread halves. Cut sandwiches into 12 small squares and skewer three onto straws. Use the packet mixes and get the kids to make their own!

BRIE, BACON AND TOMATO

Spread two slices of bread with mayonaise. Arrange thin slices of Brie on one of them. Grill three streaky bacon rashers, allow to cool before putting over the cheese. Top with tomato slices, black pepper and second slice of bread.

SCRAMBLED EGG AND CRISP

Break two eggs into a saucepan. Add a tablespoon of milk, salt and pepper and heat gently. Stir occasionally until eggs are set, but still soft. Allow to cool slightly before spreading over one slice of bread, Scatter your favourite crisps over and top with second slice.

CHAPTER SIX
WHAT'S
FOR PUD?

TREACLE TARTS

8oz/225g plain flour
4oz/100g margarine
1 egg yolk
6oz/175g porridge oats
grated rind 1 lemon
16 tbsp golden syrup

METHOD

Put flour into a bowl, add margarine and rub in
with fingertips, until mixture resembles fine
breadcrumbs. Add enough water to mix to a
firm dough. Turn onto a lightly floured surface
and knead gently. Divide into four equal pieces
and roll out until large enough to line four
4in/10cm individual flan tins (or line one larger
tin if you prefer)
Fil! each pastry case with oats and scatter
lemon rind over the top.Spoon 4 tbsp golden
syrup over each one, making sure all the oats

are covered. Use any trimming to make deco-
rations and cook at 190C/375F/Gas 5 for
25-30 mins, until cooked. Serve hot or cold
with custard or cream.
Approx cost £1.00

TIP: No oats? Use fresh breadcrumbs
instead.

APPLE AND PLUM CRUMBLE
1lb/450g cooking apples
1lb/450g plums
2oz/50g caster sugar
4oz/100g butter
4oz/100g golden syrup
6oz/175g meusli or porridge oats
2oz/50g wholemeal or plain flour

METHOD
Quarter, core and peel the apples before slic-
ing. Cut plums in half and remove stones. Cut
into slices. Layer fruit and sugar in an oven-
proof dish.
Melt the butter and syrup in a saucepan.
Remove from heat and add meusli and flour.
Mix well and scatter over the fruit.
Press down well and cook at
190C/375F/Gas 5 for 30-40 mins until gold-
en brown.
Approx cost £ 2.00

TIP: Turn those autumn windfalls into this scrumptious pud, and if you have no plums use pears instead. Fruit trees often produce more than their growers can use, so take advantage of offers from friends, roadside bargains and local fetes.

PEACH UPSIDE DOWN PUD

1 410g can sliced peaches
4 glace cherries, halved and thinly sliced
6oz/175g margarine
6oz/175g caster sugar
3 eggs, beaten
6oz/175g self-raising flour
2 tsp ground ginger

METHOD

Lightly grease and line an 8in/20cm round spring-release flan tin. Arrange the peach slices and cherries on the bottom and drizzle a little juice over.

Beat the margarine and sugar together until light and fluffy. Add the eggs a little at a time, beating well after each addition. Sift in the flour and ginger and fold in with a metal spoon. Add a little peach juice if necessary.

Spoon mixture over the peaches and level the top. Cook at 190C/375F/Gas 5 for 20-30 mins, until sponge springs back when pressed with a finger. Allow to cool slightly before turn-

ing out onto a plate, so the peaches are now on top. Serve with custard or cream
Approx cost £ 1.10

TIP: Buy peach halves if they are cheaper and cut into slices yourself. Peach slices are often thick enough to cut in half again to completely cover the base of the tin.

QUEEN OF PUDS
4 eggs
1 pint/600ml milk
4oz/100g fresh
breadcrumbs
4 tbsp strawberry
or raspberry jam
3oz/75g caster
sugar

METHOD
Separate three of the
eggs and reserve the
whites in another bowl.
Mix 3 yolks with the remaining egg. Add milk and mix well before stirring in the breadcrumbs. Spread the jam over the base of a 3 pint/1-1¾ litre ovenproof dish.
Pour the milk mixture over the top and leave for 30 mins. Cook at 150C/300F/Gas 2 for 1 hour, until set.

Whisk the reserved egg whites until stiff. Add the sugar a little at a time and whisk again after each addition. Spoon the meringue on top of the pudding and return to the oven for a further 15-20 mins until lightly browned.
Approx cost £1.20

CHOCOLATE PANCAKES
8oz/225g plain flour
2 eggs, beaten
3/4 pint/450ml milk
2oz/50g butter or marg for frying
6oz/175g chocolate spread

METHOD
Put flour, eggs and a little milk in a bowl and beat together.
Gradually add remaining milk, beating well after each addition, until the batter is the consistency of double cream. (you may not need all the milk.)
Melt a small knob of butter in a 6in/15cm frying pan and add enough batter to cover the base. When the pancake has set, flip over to cook the other side. Repeat the process with remaining batter and make about 15 pancakes. Stack them in a pile with a sheet of greaseproof between them to prevent them sticking. Keep warm in the oven.
Spread each one with chocolate spread and

stack them in a pile on a serving plate. Put 2 tbsp of chocolate spread in a piping tube fitted with a fine nozzle and pipe over the top in a zig-zag pattern. or drizzle lines over with tea-spoon. Serve warm, cut into slices like a cake.
Approx cost £1.25

BAKED APPLES

4 cooking apples
2oz/50g raisins or sultanas
1 oz/25g sugar
4 tbsp golden syrup
4 small knobs butter or margarine

METHOD

Remove the core from the centre of each apple and score a line round the skin half way up the fruit, to prevent apples bursting.
Fill the central hole with dried fruit, top with a spoonful of sugar, syrup and a knob of butter. Stand apples in a shallow dish half-filled with water and cook at 190C/375F/Gas 5 for 45-60 mins, until fruit is soft. Serve hot.
Approx cost £ 1.40

CHOCOLATE BREAD AND BUTTER PUDDING

6 slices bread, crusts removed
1oz/25g butter
2oz/50g raisins or sultanas

4 tbsp chocolate and hazelnut spread
1/2 pint/300ml milk
2 eggs
1oz/25g caster sugar
1 tsp ground nutmeg

METHOD

Spread all the bread with butter and three of the slices with chocolate spread. Make into three sandwiches and cut each into four triangles. Scatter the fruit over the bottom of a shallow ovenproof dish and arrange the bread on top.

Put milk into a saucepan and bring almost to boiling point, but not allow to boil. Whisk eggs and sugar together in a bowl and pour on warm milk, stirring all the time. Strain mixture through a sieve and pour over bread. Sprinkle nutmeg over. Leave to stand for 20 mins. Cover the pudding with foil and stand in a large roasting tin half filled with boiling water. Cook at 220C/425F/Gas 7 for 30 mins. Remove foil, sprinkle with a little more sugar and cook for further 5 mins until set and golden brown.

Approx cost £ 1.80

TIP: For extra creamy taste use a half milk and half cream mixture,

LEMON MERINGUE PIE

6oz/175g plain flour
4oz/100g butter or margarine
1 egg yolk
1 tbsp caster sugar
juice and rind of 3 lemons
1/2 pint/300ml water
1 1/2oz/65g cornflour
3 eggs, separated
8oz/225g caster sugar

METHOD

Put the flour and margarine in a bowl and rub
until mixture resembles fine breadcrumbs. Add
one egg yolk, 1 tbsp caster sugar and enough
water to make a firm dough. Turn onto a lightly
floured surface and knead gently. Roll out pastry to fit an 8in/20cm fluted flan dish or ring.
Prick base with a fork and chill for 30 mins.
Cook at 200C/400F/Gas 6 for 15-20 mins,
until cooked but not browned too much.
Put rind and juice into a bowl with the cornflour. Add 2 tbsp water and mix until smooth.
Heat remaining water in a saucepan until boiling and pour onto cornflour mixture, stirring.
Return to the pan and bring gently to the boil,
stirring all the time.
Remove from heat and beat in 2 egg yolks and
3oz/75g of the sugar. Cool slightly and pour
into cooked flan case.

Whisk the egg whites until stiff. Add the sugar a little at a time, whisking well after each addition. Spoon meringue over lemon filling. Cook at 180C/350F/Gas 4 for 15-20 mins, until lightly browned. Serve warm.

Approx cost £2.00

CHOCOLATE PUDDLE PUDDING

6oz/175g self-raising flour
2oz/50g cocoa powder
1/4pint/150ml milk
2oz/50g butter or margarine, melted
5oz/125g caster sugar
1/2 tsp vanilla essence
3oz/75g soft brown sugar
2 tbsp cocoa powder
3/4 pint/450ml water

METHOD

Put flour, cocoa, milk, margarine, sugar and essence in a bowl and beat together. Transfer mixture to a 2 pint/1 litre pie dish in an even layer.
Put soft brown sugar, cocoa and water in a saucepan. Bring to the boil and pour over the pudding. Cook at 190c/375F/Gas 5 for 40-45 mins.
When served the chocolate sauce will be in the bottom of the dish.

Approx cost £ 1.50

APPLE AND MINCEMEAT ROLL

8oz/225g puff pastry
2oz/50g fresh breadcrumbs
4oz/100g mincemeat
2oz/50g chopped walnuts
8oz/225g cooking apples, peeled cored and
sliced
grated rind 1 orange
2oz/50g butter, melted

METHOD

Roll pastry out on a lightly floured surface to
make a large thin rectangle.
Mix breadcrumbs, mincemeat, nuts, apples
and orange rind together and spread over the
rectangle, leaving a 1/2inch/1cm border round
the edges. Brush edges with melted butter and
roll up like a Swiss roll. Seal ends.
Lift onto a lightly greased baking sheet and
brush with remaining butter. Cook at
200C/400F/Gas 6 for 25-30 mins until risen
and golden brown. Dust with a little icing sugar
before serving.
Approx cost £2.20

PEAR LAYER PUD

8oz/225g fresh breadcrumbs
2lb/1kg ripe pears, peeled, cored and sliced
4oz/100g brown sugar
2oz/50g butter

METHOD

Lightly grease and line an 8in/20cm dish. Cover the base with 2oz/50g of the breadcrumbs. Arrange a third of the pears in a layer on top. Repeat layers finishing with a layer of pears. Dot with butter and cook at 190C/375F/Gas 5 for 40-45 mins, until pears are tender. Sprinkle with icing sugar before serving while still warm.

Approx cost £1.60

TIP: Use drained, canned pears if they are cheaper.

GOOSEBERRY AND APPLE MERINGUES

8oz/225g gooseberries, topped and tailed
8oz/225g cooking apples, peeled, cored and sliced
1 tbsp water
1oz/25g butter
5oz/125g sugar
$1/2$oz/15g fresh breadcrumbs
2 eggs separated
$1/2$ tsp mixed spice

METHOD

Put gooseberries, apples, water and butter in a saucepan and simmer for 10 mins, until tender. Remove from heat and mix in 1oz/25g sugar, breadcrumbs, egg yolks and mixed spice.

Lightly grease four ramekin dishes and fill with apple mixture. Stand on a baking sheet and cook at 180C/350F/Gas 4 for 15-20 mins, until set.

Whisk egg whites until stiff and fold in the remaining sugar a little at a time. Whisk again. Spoon or pipe meringue over the fruit filled ramekins. Reduce heat of oven to 140C/275F/Gas 1 and return fruity desserts to the oven for further 30 mins, until meringue is golden brown. Serve immediately.

Approx cost £1.75

TIP: Use bottled or canned gooseberries when they are out of season.

BOOZY BANANAS

4 bananas, peeled and sliced
1 227g can pineapple pieces in natural juice
2oz/50g raisins
2 tbsp lemon juice
12 tsp mixed spice
2 tbsp brown sugar
4 tbsp rum (optional)

METHOD

Put sliced bananas in a shallow pan with the pineapple and juice, raisins, lemon juice, spice, sugar and rum. Heat gently and simmer for 15-20 mins, until fruit has softened. Serve with whipped cream.

Approx cost £ 1.60

STEAMED CHOCOLATE PUDDING

4oz/100g plain chocolate
6oz/175g butter
6oz/175g soft brown sugar
2 eggs, beaten
5oz/125g self raising flour
2 tbsp cocoa powder
1 oz/25g fresh breadcrumbs
3 tbsp milk

METHOD

Lightly grease a 2 pint/1 litre pudding basin. Break chocolate into pieces and put in a bowl over a pan of hot, but not boiling, water and allow to melt. Beat butter and sugar together until light and fluffy. Beat in melted chocolate and then the eggs, a little at a time.
Sift in flour and cocoa and fold in with breadcrumbs. Add enough milk to give a dropping consistency.

Turn into basin, level the top and cover with a double layer of greaseproof paper. Cover with foil and tie a string handle round. Place on a trivet in a large pan half filled with boiling water, cover and steam for 2 $\frac{1}{2}$ hours, topping up with more water when necessary.

CHOCOLATE SAUCE

3oz/75g caster sugar
8oz/225g bar plain chocolate
1oz/25g butter

METHOD

Put sugar in a small pan with 8 tbsp water and simmer until dissolved. Remove from heat and add chocolate, broken into pieces, and butter. Stir well until melted before pouring over sponge.

Run a knife round the edge to loose pudding and turn onto a serving plate. Serve with chocolate sauce, custard or cream.

Approx cost £2.40 (with chocolate sauce)

OLD FASHIONED RICE PUDDING

2oz/50g pudding rice
2oz/50g caster sugar
1 pint/600ml milk
1/2 pint/300ml single cream
grated rind 1 lemon
knob butter
1 tsp ground nutmeg

METHOD

Put rice and sugar in a 2
pint/1 litre ovenproof dish
and stand on a baking sheet.
Heat the milk and cream gently in a
saucepan, add lemon and bring to boiling
point. Pour over the rice and stir well. Add butter and sprinkle with nutmeg. Cook at
170C/325F/Gas 3 for 2 hours, stirring once
during the first hour.
Approx cost £1.10

EGG CUSTARD TART

8oz/225g plain flour
5oz/125g butter or margarine
5 eggs
1oz/25g caster sugar
1 pint/600ml milk
few drops vanilla essence
2 tsp ground nutmeg

METHOD

Put flour and fat in a bowl and rub in until mixture resembles fine breadcrumbs. Add one egg yolk and enough water to make a firm dough. Turn onto a lightly floured surface and knead gently. Roll out until large enough to line an 8inch/20cm deep-sided flan tin. Prick the base with a fork and chill for 30 mins. Cook at 200C/400F/Gas 6 for 15-20 mins until lightly browned.

Whisk 4 eggs, sugar and essence together. Warm milk to blood heat and whisk into eggs. Strain through a sieve into the cooked pastry case. Sprinkle nutmeg over the top and cook at 180C/350F/Gas 4 for 35-40 mins, until set and browned. Serve warm.

Approx cost £ 1.70

TIP: Line pastry case with crumpled foil, baking beans or smaller dish to prevent the sides collapsing during cooking time. Remove flan case from oven after 15 mins when the pastry will be firm. Lift out foil, or whatever and return the empty case to the oven for further 5 mins to finish cooking.

JAM LAYER PUDDING

12oz/350g plain flour
6oz/175g beef suet
1 454g jar red jam of your choice

METHOD

Put the flour and suet in a bowl and stir
together. Add enough water to make a firm
dough. Turn onto a lightly floured surface and
knead gently. Divide into seven equal balls.
Lightly grease a 1 pint/600ml pudding basin.
Put a spoonful of jam in the base and flatten
one ball of suet on top of it.
Spread with more jam. Knead 1 1/2 balls
together and flatten to make a second layer.
Spread with more jam. Knead 2 balls together
for the third layer and top with jam. Knead
remaining balls 2 1/2 balls together to make
the final layer.
Cover with a double layer of greaseproof paper
and then cover with foil. Tie string round to
make a handle and stand on a trivet in a pan of
boiling water.
Cover and steam for 3 hours, topping up with
more boiling water when necessary.
Turn out onto a serving plate.
Serve hot with custard.
Approx cost £1.00

SWEET BATTER PUDDING

3 tbsp plain flour
3 eggs, beaten
5 tbsp caster sugar
3/4 pint/450ml milk
2oz/50g butter
1 425g can black cherries, drained

METHOD

Put flour into a bowl and add eggs. Beat well
and stir in 3 tbsp sugar.
Heat milk until blood heat and pour into the
egg mixture.
Lightly grease a shallow ovenproof dish and
arrange cherries over the base. Pour the batter over and dot with butter. Cook at
220C/425F/Gas 7 for 30-35 mins, until
risen and browned. Dust with a little caster
sugar before serving.
Approx cost £1.75

CABINET PUDDING

6 trifle sponges, cut into cubes
2oz/50g glace cherries, chopped
1oz/25g caster sugar
2 eggs, beaten
1 pint/600ml milk
few drops vanilla flavouring

METHOD

Toss the sponges, cherries and sugar together in a bowl.

Beat eggs, milk and essence together and pour over the sponges. Leave to stand for 45 mins.

Lightly grease a 1^1/2 pint/900ml pudding basin and turn the mixture into it. Press down and cover with a double layer of greaseproof paper before covering with foil. Toe a string handle round and stand on a trivet in a pan half filled with boiling water. Cover and steam for an hour, topping up with more water when necessary. Lift out carefully and turn out onto a plate. Serve with custard or cream.

Approx cost £1.50

TROPICAL FRUIT CRUMBLE

6oz/175g plain flour
3oz/75g butter or margarine
3oz/75g white or demerara sugar
1 tsp ground cinnamon
1 227g can pineapple pieces
1 410g can peach slices
2 bananas, sliced

METHOD

Put flour and butter in a bowl and rub in fat with fingertips, until mixture resembles fine breadcrumbs. Stir in sugar and spices.

Drain fruit and arrange in an ovenproof dish, with a little of the juice. Scatter crumble mixture over the top and pat down. Cook at 190C/375F/Gas 5 for 45-50 mins, until browned.

Approx cost £ 1.40

AUTUMN PUDDING

1lb/450g cooking apples, peeled cored and sliced
8oz/225g blackberries
2oz/50g caster sugar
8 thin slices bread, crusts removed

METHOD

Stew apples and 4oz/100g blackberries with a little water and sugar until soft. Allow to cool.
Cut a circle from one of the slices of bread, large enough to cover the base of a 1 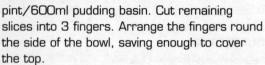 pint/600ml pudding basin. Cut remaining slices into 3 fingers. Arrange the fingers round the side of the bowl, saving enough to cover the top.
When the fruit is cool strain and reserve the juice. Stir in whole blackberries. Moisten the

bread with the strained juice and fill bowl with fruit. Top with remaining bread and press down well. Cover with a plate, put a weight on the top and chill overnight in the fridge.
To serve, loosen the edges with a knife and turn out onto a plate

Approx cost £1.00

TIP: Pick the blackberries when out walking. Soak in cold water to remove any insects and drain on kitchen paper. Add fruit to apples and freeze the rest. Arrange in a single layer on a baking sheet and open freeze. Tip into a polybag and seal. The fruit will then flow freely and won't be stuck together in one big lump.

SHOO FLY PIE
10oz/300g plain flour
5oz/125g margarine
1 tsp caster sugar
4oz/100g raisins
4oz/100g brown sugar
1/2 tsp bicarbonate of soda
2 tsp mixed spice

METHOD

Put 6oz/175g plain flour in a bowl with
3oz/75g margarine. Rub in with fingertips,
until mixture resembles fine breadcrumbs. Stir
in caster sugar and add water to make a firm
dough. Turn onto a lightly floured surface and
knead gently. Roll out until large enough to line
an 8in/20cm flan dish. Prick base with a fork.
Scatter raisins over the base. Mix 2oz/50g
brown sugar with bicarb and 4 tbsp hot water.
Pour over the dried fruit.

Put remaining 4oz/100g plain flour in a bowl
with 2oz/50g margarine and rub in fat until
mixture resembles fine breadcrumbs. Stir in
remaining brown sugar and mixed spice.
Sprinkle over the flan and cook at
200C/400F/Gas 6 for 15 mins. Turn heat
down to 170C/325F/Gas 3 for further 20-25
mins. Serve warm or cold.

Approx cost £1.25

COLD DESSERTS

CASSATA
1 litre pack raspberry ripple ice cream
1/2 litre brick vanilla ice cream
2oz/50g raisins
2oz/50g glace cherries
2oz/50g chocolate drops

METHOD
Chill a 2 pint/1 litre pudding basin.
Allow the raspberry ice cream to soften slightly
and spread it over the base and up the sides
of the pudding basin in an even layer. Don't
worry if it isn't too neat. Put it back into the
freezer to harden.

Put vanilla ice cream in a bowl and beat in raisins, cherries and chocolate drops. Take the basin out of the freezer and smooth raspberry ice cream with the back of a spoon. Fill the centre with the vanilla mixture. Level the top and return to the freezer to harden.

Dip the bowl briefly into hot water and run a warm knife round the edge of the cassatta to loosen it. Turn out onto a plate. Smooth sides and return to the freezer until required.

Approx cost £ 1.60

CREME CARAMEL

85 ml/3fl oz water
6 1/2 oz/180g caster sugar
1 pint/600ml milk
few drops vanilla essence
2 eggs, beaten
2 egg yolks

METHOD

Put water in a saucepan with 4oz/100g caster sugar and heat gently, without stirring. Bring to the boil and and simmer gently until golden brown. Share caramel between four warmed ramekin dishes and turn quickly to coat the base and sides. Leave to cool.

Put the milk and vanilla essence in a pan and bring to the boil. Remove from heat and stir in remaining 2 1/2oz/65g sugar, leave to dissolve. Lightly beat eggs and egg yolks together and add to milk. Stir well. Strain through a sieve into the ramekin dishes.

Place the dishes in a roasting tin half-filled with boiling water. Cover with foil and cook at 180C/350F/Gas 4 for 45-50 mins, until custard is set and a knife inserted comes out clean.

Lift out of the water and leave to cool. Chill for at least an hour and preferably overnight before serving. Run a knife round the edge to loosen custard and turn carefully onto a plate, allowing the caramel to coat the pudding.

Approx cost £1.20

FRUITY MERINGUE

4 egg whites
8oz/225g caster sugar
4 tsp cornflour
1 tsp vinegar
1/2 tsp vanilla essence
1/2 pint/300ml double cream
2 kiwi fruit, peeled and sliced
8oz/225g strawberries

METHOD

Line a baking sheet with baking parchment. Beat egg whites until stiff. Add sugar a little at a time, whisking well after each addition. Beat in cornflour, vinegar and essence. Spoon mix-

ture onto the baking parchment and spread
out to make a large circle. Cook at
140C/275F/Gas 1 for 1 1/2 hours. The
paper should peel off easily if the meringue is
cooked. Leave to cool. The mixture will crack
slightly and that is a feature of this meringue.
Carefully peel off the paper and put meringue
onto serving platter.
Whip the cream until thick but still floppy and
spread over meringue.
Halve strawberries and scatter fruit over the
top with the sliced kiwi.
Approx cost £ 2.50

TIP: Use the same mixture to make 2 smaller circles that can be sandwiched together
with the cream, or make four individual
desserts. Use any soft fruit to top meringue,
depending on what is in season and therefore
cheaper. Try bananas, canned pineapple
chunks, raspberries or sliced plums.

APRICOT CREAMS

1 411g can apricot halves in natural juice,
drained
2oz/50g brown sugar
1/2 pint/300ml double
cream
1/4 pint/150ml natural
yogurt

METHOD

Roughly chop apricots and put in a saucepan
with a little juice and 2 tbsp of brown sugar.
Simmer gently for 5-10 mins. Allow to cool and
share between four glasses, pouring over a little of the syrup.

Whip the cream until thick but still slightly floppy. Stir in yogurt and mix well. Spoon mixture
over apricots. Sprinkle the rest of the sugar
over the four desserts and chill overnight.

Approx cost £ 1.50

LEMON GINGER CHEESECAKE

4oz/100g margarine
8oz/225g ginger biscuits, crushed
4oz/100g sugar
rind and juice of 2 lemons
1 11g sachet gelatin
10oz/275g cottage cheese, sieved
1/2 pint/300ml whipping cream
2 tsp ground ginger

METHOD

Lightly grease and line an 8in/20cm spring
release flan tin.

Melt margarine in a pan, add biscuits and half
the sugar and mix well. Use the back of a
spoon to spread half the mixture in an even
layer over the base of the tin. Chill.

Put lemon juice in a small bowl. Stand in a pan

half filled with simmering water. Sprinkle
gelatin over, mix well and leave until dissolved,
stirring occasionally.

Put cottage cheese. lemon rind, caster sugar,
cream and ginger in a bowl and mix well. Fold
in the gelatin and juice. Spoon mixture into the
tin and level top. Scatter remaining crumbs in
an even layer over the top. Press down and
chill for at least 3 hours, or until set.

Dust lightly with icing sugar before serving.

Approx cost £2.50

QUICK CHOCOLATE MOUSSE

6oz/175g plain chocolate
rind and juice 1 orange
1/2oz/15g butter
3 eggs, separated
1 tbsp instant coffee, dissolved
in 1 tbsp boiling water

METHOD

Grate a little of the chocolate and reserve for
decoration

Break the rest of the chocolate into a bowl
over a pan of hot, but not boiling water, and
leave to melt. Stir in orange rind.

Remove from heat and beat in the egg yolks, 1
tbsp orange juice and coffee.

Whisk egg whites until stiff and fold them into
the chocolate mixture. Divide between four

glasses, top with reserved grated chocolate
and chill.
Approx cost £1.30

APRICOT TART

6oz/175g plain flour
3oz/75g margarine
1 egg yolk
2 eggs
1 1/2oz/40g caster sugar
3/4 oz/20g cornflour
1/4 pint/150ml milk, plus 5 tbsp for mixing
1/2 tsp vanilla essence
2 x 411g cans apricot halves
6 tbsp apricot jam

METHOD

Put flour and margarine in a bowl and rub in
fat with fingertips, until mixture resembles fine
breadcrumbs. Add egg yolk and enough water
to mix to a firm dough. Roll out to fit an
8in/20cm flan tin . Prick base with a fork and
chill for 30 mins. Cook at 200C/400F/Gas 6
for 20-25 mins until lightly browned and
cooked.
Beat eggs and sugar together in a basin. Add
cornflour and 5 tbsp of milk and mix again.
Heat remaining milk in a pan until almost boiling. Pour onto the eggs, stirring all the time.
Pour back into the pan and return to the heat.

Bring gently to the boil, still stirring all the time, until thickened. Add vanilla essence, stir again and cover tightly with cling film to prevent a skin forming while it cools.

Spread over cooled flan case.

Drain fruit and arrange on top of custard.

Heat apricot jam until runny. Sieve to remove lumps and brush a thick layer of jam over the apricots. Chill.

Approx cost £2.00

RASPBERRY MOUSSE

1 300g can raspberries
1 pack raspberry jelly, cut into cubes
1 410g can evaporated milk, chilled
1 tsp lemon juice
4 tbsp double or whipping cream

METHOD

Strain juice from raspberries into a measuring jug and top up to $1/2$ pint/300ml with water if necessary. Put into a saucepan with the jelly. Heat gently until jelly dissolves.

Transfer to a bowl and chill until just starting to set.

Push the raspberries through a sieve to remove pips.

Put evaporated milk and lemon juice into a bowl and whisk until it stands in soft peaks.

Fold in the sieved raspberries and the jelly. Mix well and spoon into a bowl or individual dishes and chill until set.

Whip the cream until thick but still floppy and use to decorate the mousse.

Approx cost £2.20

LAYERED APPLE PUDDING

3oz/75g butter or margarine
8oz/225g fresh breadcrumbs
2 oz/50g white or demerara sugar
1 1/2lbs/675g cooking apples, peeled, cored and sliced
rind and juice 1 lemon
2oz/50g caster sugar
1/2 pint/300ml double or whipping cream

METHOD

Melt butter in a frying pan, add breadcrumbs and fry until crisp and golden brown . Remove from heat and stir in sugar.

Meanwhile put apples in a saucepan with the lemon rind and juice, sugar and a little water and cook until tender. Leave to cool.

Put half the apples in a serving dish and level.

Spread half the breadcrumbs on top. Add
another layer of apple and top with a layer of
breadcrumbs.
Whip the cream until thick but still floppy and
use to decorate the top. Chill, serve as soon
as possible before crumbs go too soggy.
Approx cost £1.80

PROFITEROLES AND CHOCOLATE SAUCE

¼ pint/150ml water
2oz/50g butter
2 ½oz/65g plain flour
2 eggs, beaten
¼ pint/150ml whipping or double cream
8oz/225g icing sugar
3 tsp cocoa powder
2-4 tbsp water

METHOD

Put water and butter into a saucepan, allow
butter to melt and bring to boiling point.
Remove from heat. Tip all the flour in at once
and beat quickly until mixture leaves the sides
of the pan clean.Leave to cool for
10 mins.
Add the eggs to the mixture,
a little at a time, beating
well after each addition, until
mixture is thick and glossy.

You may not need all the egg.
Dampen a baking sheet and arrange walnut-sized spoonfuls of the mixture on it, leaving space to rise. Cook at 220C/425F/Gas 7 for 25-30 mins, until well-risen and golden.
Remove from oven and make a small split in the side of each one to allow steam to escape and prevent them going soggy.
Whip the cream until thick and put a teaspoonful inside each bun.
Sift icing sugar and cocoa into a bowl. Add enough water to make a thick glossy icing.
Stack buns in a pile and drizzle some of the sauce over. Serve the rest in a jug for pouring.
Approx cost £1.25

RED FRUIT CRUMBLE

1 560g can red plums
1 406g can strawberries
8oz/225g leftover sponge cake
2 tbsp ground almonds
1 tbsp sugar

METHOD

Pour fruit into an ovenproof dish. Crumble cake and mix with almonds and sugar. Scatter over fruit and cook at 200C/400F/Gas 6 for 10-15 mins
Approx cost £ 1.50

BANANA FLAN

4oz/125g caster sugar
6 tbsp cornflour
3/4pint/450ml milk
3 egg yolks, beaten
few drops vanilla essence
4oz/100g butter, melted
6oz/175g ginger biscuits, crushed
rind and juice 1 lemon
4 bananas, sliced
1/4 pint/150ml double or whipping cream

METHOD

Lightly grease an 8inch/20cm shallow flan
dish.
Put sugar, cornflour and milk in a saucepan.
Bring to the boil, stirring until mixture thickens.
Remove from heat and beat in egg yolks, vanilla essence and 1 tbsp of the melted butter.
Return to heat and cook for 1 min, but don't
boil.
Lift off heat and cover tightly with cling film.
Leave to cool.
Stir biscuit crumbs into remaining melted butter. Add lemon rind and use the back of a
spoon to spread the mixture over the base and
sides of the flan tin, pressing down well. Chill
until set.
Toss the sliced bananas in lemon juice to prevent discolouration and arrange half of them

over the base of the biscuit case. Cover with a
thin layer of custard. Add another layer of
bananas, reserving a few for decoration.
Whip the cream until thick but still floppy and
stir into the remaining custard. Spoon over the
top of the flan and top with reserved bananas.
Chill.

Approx cost £2.50

SCORCHED RASPBERRY CREAMS

8oz/225g fresh raspberries, or 1 300g can,
drained
1 pint/450ml double cream
1 tsp vanilla essence
4 tbsp demerara sugar

METHOD

Share the fruit between four ramekins or scatter over the base of a shallow, heatproof dish.
Whip the cream until thick but still floppy and
spoon over the fruit. Chill for 2 hours. Remove
from fridge and sprinkle the top with a thick
layer of demerara sugar. Heat the grill until
very hot and pop dishes under
for a minute or two, until sugar
starts to melt. Cool and chill
for further 2hours
before serving.

Approx cost £2.20

TOUTE SUITE TRIFLE

6 trifle sponges
4 tbsp jam
1 300g can raspberries
1 532g carton ready to serve custard
1oz/25g flaked almonds, toasted
¼ pint/150ml double or whipping cream
(optional)

METHOD

Split the sponges and spread with jam.
Sandwich together again and arrange in the
bottom of a glass bowl. Drain raspberries and
drizzle the juice over the sponges. Scatter fruit
over the sponge. Pour custard over and chill.
Decorate with toasted nuts, and cream if
desired. Chill.
Approx cost £ 1.95

TIP: use canned sliced peaches if they are
special offer. Roughly chop the fruit but save
some to decorate the top.

PORTUGUESE ORANGE ROLL

1 tbsp cornflour
¼ pint/150ml orange juice
7oz/200g caster sugar
grated rind 1 orange
5 eggs, beaten

METHOD

Lightly grease and line a 12x8in/30x20cm
Swiss roll tin. Grease the paper and sprinkle
with a little caster sugar
Put the cornflour in a bowl and stir in the
orange juice. Add sugar, rind and eggs and
mix well. Pour the mixture into the prepared tin
and cook at 180C/350F Gas 4 for 15-20
mins, until firm. Turn out onto a damp cloth,
also sprinkled with sugar, trim edges and roll
up carefully, using the cloth to help lift the roll.
Transfer to a serving dish, sprinkle with a little
more sugar and chill.
Approx cost £ 1.50

FLUMMERY

¹/2 pint/300ml double cream
1 tbsp clear honey
1 tsp whisky (optional)
1 tbsp lemon juice
1 oz/25g porridge oats

METHOD

Whip the cream until thick but still floppy.
Heat the honey until it's runny and mix with the
whisky and lemon juice. Toast the porridge
until lightly browned. Stir the honey mixture
into the cream and share between four glasses. Top with toasted oats and serve.
Approx cost £ 1.20

RICE CONDE

2oz/50g pudding rice
1/2 pint/300ml milk
grated rind and juice of 1 lemon
1oz/25g caster sugar
1/4 pint/150ml double cream
1/4 pint/150ml natural yogurt

METHOD

Put rice and milk into a saucepan. Add lemon
rind and bring to the boil. Reduce heat, cover
and simmer for about 1 hour, stirring occasionally, until rice is soft. Stir in sugar and allow
to cool.
Whip the cream until thick but still floppy. Add
lemon juice to rice mixture and fold in whipped
cream and yogurt. Share between four glasses
and chill. Top with fresh fruit or toasted nuts, if
desired, before serving.
Approx cost £ 1.30

ORANGE SORBET

4oz/100g caster sugar
1/2 pint/300ml water
4 large oranges
1 tbsp lemon juice
2 egg whites

METHOD

Put sugar and water in a saucepan and heat gently, until sugar has dissolved. Bring to the boil simmer for 15 mins, remove from heat and allow to cool.

Use a canelle knife or zester to remove strips of skin from the oranges and reserve for decoration. Cut the top off the oranges and use a sharp knife to remove as much flesh as possible from inside. Discard all pips and membranes. Reserve the shells.

Add flesh and lemon juice to sugar mixture and turn into a polybox and freeze until mushy. Remove from freezer. Whisk egg whites until stiff and fold into sorbet mixture.

Cut a thin slice off the base of the orange shells so they can stand on their own and fill with the sorbet. Freeze until firm. Transfer to the fridge one hour before serving to allow to defrost slightly. Top with orange rind and 'lid'.

Approx cost £1.00

CHOCOLATE ROULADE

1oz/25g cocoa powder
1/4 pint/150ml milk
4 eggs, separated
4oz/100g caster sugar
1/2 pint/300ml double cream
8oz/225g fresh strawberries

METHOD

Grease and line an 12x8in/30x20cm Swiss
roll tin.
Mix cocoa and milk together in a small pan and
heat gently until cocoa has dissolved
Remove from heat and allow to cool.
Put egg yolks and sugar in a bowl over a pan of
simmering water and whisk together until pale
and fluffy. The whisk should leave a trail of mixture when lifted.
Remove from heat and whisk in cooled cocoa
mixture,
Whisk egg whites in another bowl until stiff.
Fold cocoa mixture carefully into egg whites
and pour into prepared tin. Cook at
180C/350F/Gas 4 for 20 mins, until sponge
is firm to the touch.
Turn sponge out onto a piece of greaseproof
paper sprinkled with sugar, cover with a warm,
damp tea towel and leave to cool for 20 mins.
Use the tea towel to help roll up the sponge.
Whip the cream until thick but still floppy.

Reserve half to decorate the top. Roughly chop
half the fruit and stir into whipped cream.
Unroll the sponge and spread cream and fruit
mixture over. Roll up again and transfer to
serving plate.
Spoon or pipe remaining cream along the
top.Slice remaining strawberries and arrange
in the cream. Chill before serving.

Approx cost £2.00

New Authors and Manuscripts welcome.
We reply to all correspondence.

If you wish the return of your
manuscript please enclose a SAE.

Correspondence to:
Harlequin Books Limited
Barn Oast,
Woodfalls Industrial Estate,
Gravelly Way,
Laddingford,
Kent ME18 6DA

HARLEQUIN
BOOKS LIMITED

Barn Oast, Woodfalls Industrial Estate, Gravelly Way,
Laddingford, Kent ME18 6DA